VACHEL LINDSAY
ADVENTURER

NICHOLAS VACHEL LINDSAY

VACHEL LINDSAY,
Adventurer

By

ALBERT EDMUND TROMBLY

Columbia, Mo.
LUCAS BROTHERS
1929

Copyright, 1929,
LUCAS BROTHERS.

Printed in the United States of America.

To the Friend, unnamed but unforgotten, who, six years ago, made clear the meaning of friendship.

CONTENTS

	Page
Chapter I—Biographical	1
Chapter II—The Prose Books	47
Chapter III—The Poems	85
Chapter IV—The Picture Books	125
Chapter V—Conclusion	146
Bibliography	156

ILLUSTRATIONS

	Page
Nicholas Vachel Lindsay	Frontispiece
The Poet's Parents	8
Map of The Universe	144

FOREWORD

If a study undertaken during the subject's productivity must be incomplete and tentative, it may still be serviceable for the data which it offers. Information available while a man and his friends are living may be out of reach after his and their death. So this little book, of no great moment now, may be helpful to later students of Mr. Lindsay.

The writer is sincerely grateful to all who have helped to make his study possible. Mr. Lindsay's family and friends have given invaluable and unstinted help especially in the preparation of the biographical chapter. For much relating to the poet's childhood use has been made of a brief unpublished sketch left by his mother. Parts of it have been quoted almost verbatim, others paraphrased.

Acknowledgment is due to The Macmillan Company for permission to quote from those of Mr. Lindsay's books which they publish and to reproduce the *Map of The Universe,* and to D. Appleton & Company for permission to quote from *Going-To-The-Stars* and *The Candle In The Cabin.*

A part of chapter two appeared as an essay in the *Southwest Review,* and is reprinted here with the permission of the editors.

CHAPTER I

Biographical

Mr. Lindsay likes to think of himself as an adventurer; and there must be few of his contemporaries whose adventures have been as numerous and varied as his. He has tramped across a fair number of the United States, delved into Egyptian hieroglyphics, laid down the law for the motion-picture, preached the gospel of beauty, scrambled over the Rockies, drawn pictures and made books, and thundered the *Congo* at academic gatherings and in London drawing-rooms. But more significant than many of these, was his first adventure: his advent in the Lindsay family.

A poet is neither a divine gift nor an incomprehensible accident; rather is he a sociological effect (a retribution, perhaps!) for which there have been certain, if sometimes remote and intangible causes. The parents who looked upon their strange son with misgivings, who could not seem to account for him, who would have preferred a physician to a poet, needed only to examine themselves more closely if they would understand him. He is, after all, very much what they made him. No one realizes this better than he; and he says wisely in one of his prefaces that he does not expect to get very far away from the boy he was at six years of age. If we glance into the Lindsay household we may see something of what tended to shape the boy's peculiar talent, and we may even surmise why a poet should have been loosed on this particular family.

The Lindsays are of Scotch origin. On the maternal side of the poet's family, the Frazees, Austens, and Doniphans are of Scotch and English ancestry with a mixture of Welsh and Spanish. The poet tells us of an aunt's suspicions that the family had an Indian among its ancestors; and he delights in adding that if there was one such ancestor, there were a million of them naturally! Mr. Lindsay's paternal grandfather had been a large landholder in Kentucky before the Civil War. His sympathies were with the South, though he was an avowed adherent of the Union. During the war his land was devastated, his horses were stolen, he and his family left empty-handed. It remained for his oldest son Vachel Thomas (1844-1918), the poet's father, to rehabilitate the family fortunes; and he assumed the task with courage and energy. He paid his way through the Miami Medical College and helped his brothers and sisters to a start in business or an education. Once launched in his profession, he took it very seriously and made the most of it. He spent a year abroad in the hospitals of Dresden and Vienna. Medicine became in his eyes the highest possible calling, and, on one occasion, when the pastor of the congregation to which the Lindsays belonged decided to give up the ministry to study medicine, Dr. Lindsay assured him that he was going one step higher.

He was a large, strong, black-bearded man, impulsive and resolute, quick-moving and surmounting obstacles with sheer physical strength. He was a fanatical prohibitionist, a man who never used tobacco and who did not believe that his children should dance or play cards. A Democrat, a transplanted Kentuckian, he retained his Southern ways and prejudices. He did not share in the enhusiasm of his wife and children for Lincoln; and, in fact, never quite forgave him the invasion of the South, the freeing of the slaves, and the impoverishment of Southern families which made it necessary for young gentlemen to earn a livelihood.

The struggle which Dr. Lindsay had known had made him profoundly respectful of money and of the practical. Yet he was neither hard nor shrewd. He wore himself out in the service of his family and his clients.

He reared his children in comfort, gave them all a college education, and denied them none of what he thought to be wholesome pleasures. He was fond of travel and on several occasions took his wife and, once at least, his children to Europe. Then there were frequent summer vacations in the Colorado mountains; and, towards the end of his life, the doctor and Mrs. Lindsay visited China.

Family life meant much to him. He was fond of telling his children the stories and singing them the songs which he had heard in his childhood from Negro maids. He liked to read them *Uncle Remus,* too, and to take them to minstrel shows. Singing he enjoyed, for he possessed a good resonant voice. Friends who knew the doctor's letters, written from abroad or from the Colorado mountains, speak of their humor and charm.

Catherine Frazee (1848-1922), the poet's mother, came of a family which trailed into Indiana the glory of its Virginian ancestors.

One of her great uncles was Colonel William Doniphan who had distinguished himself as commander of the Missouri troops during the Mexican war. Preachers were frequent in the family, and Mrs. Lindsay's father was the farmer and preacher whom his grandson celebrates in *The Proud Farmer*.

"Into the acres of the newborn state.

He poured his strength and plowed his ancient name."

Six days in the week this energetic pioneer tilled the soil, after having held morning prayers for his family and hired hands, and on the seventh he preached in the village church. His daughter gave clear proof of her moral fibre during her college career. She had suffered a sunstroke which left her virtually blind for several years; yet, in spite of the handicap, she got her sisters, who were fellow-students, to read aloud to her, and when she graduated from Glendale College, it was as valedictorian. After graduation she taught painting and English literature at Glendale and later at Hocker College (now part of the University of Kentucky). One of her colleagues and friends at Hocker was Miss Eudora Lindsay. Having taught a while, the two girls decided to take a year off abroad. It happened that Dr. Vachel T. Lindsay, Eudora's brother, had chosen the same year for his study in European hospitals; so the three sailed together, and Miss Frazee and the doctor met for the first time on shipboard. Europe became their courting-ground, and the romance which carried them from the galleries of Dresden to those of Italy, became and remained the dominant fact in their lives. Shortly after their return to America, they were married.

During the year abroad the two girls wrote up their experiences, in the form of letters, for weeklies at home; and later Miss Lindsay collected and published her contributions in a book, which, as her nephew says, became a sort of family bible.* To readers of today, cloyed with the lurid and sensational, the Lindsay "family bible" might seem a quaint and refreshing old book. It has something of the inevitable didactic tone, but the letters descriptive of Europe are full of shrewd observation and humor.

With marriage Mrs. Lindsay's sphere of activities only broadened. She bore six children of whom three are now living. She belonged to a generation of women who still took pride in being good cooks, energetic housekeepers, and desirable neighbors. She was neither large nor strong physically, but possessed boundless nervous energy of which she made the utmost use. She was an ardent temperance advocate, a Sunday school teacher for many years, and originator of a union of the Women's Missionary Societies of all the churches in Springfield and president of it for thirty years, until her

*Wayside Notes And Fireside Thoughts, by Eudora. John Burns Publishing Company, St. Louis, 1884.

The Poet's Parents

VACHEL THOMAS LINDSAY   CATHERINE FRAZEE LINDSAY

death. This union was her crowning achievement as a church worker. Her study abroad, at a time when that sort of thing was far less common than it is today, gave her a certain distinction, and she was called upon often to lecture on the European masters of painting and letters. On at least two occasions she wrote and staged masque-like productions; and her son takes roguish delight in remembering that these rather pagan plays were performed in the church and that the goddess Venus, one of the characters, was perched in the pulpit. He is glad to acknowledge, too, that the dialogue of one of the plays—in all likelihood *The Colloquy Of The Nations*—may have suggested the nature and form of his *Litany Of The Heroes*.

In 1920 when Mrs. Lindsay was shattered in health with brooding over the death of her husband, her son thought to distract and comfort her with a short visit to England. England to her was an old haunt, and the trip became a sort of triumphal march. Half blind and half in the grave as she was, she discussed shrewdly and convincingly poetry, art, men, and books; and everywhere the people with whom she talked realized that they had come in contact with an extraordinary woman.

Lovers of the home and of the homely virtues, the Lindsays had a large capacity for youth. The romance which had begun in the European art galleries only ripened with the years. To friends and relatives their life was an inspiration. In their last years, when on their way to China, a woman on board stepped up to Mrs. Lindsay and said: "You and the doctor have just been married, haven't you?"

Energy, self-reliance, that determination which we sometimes call hard-headedness, an unquestioning adherence to much of what is disparaged today as puritanism, a pious attitude towards life, a love of oratory, the poet got from both parents. From his

Biographical

father he got his booming voice; but by one of those jokes which life seems to delight in playing, the son of a practical and thrifty father became a man for whom verse-making and the open road had more meaning than did money. To his mother, and he is decidedly his mother's child, he owes his utopianism, his bent for reform, his tendency to seek self-articulation in drawing and verbal expression.

Most men never venture out of the narrow circle which their forebears have traced around them; but now and then a restless and irrepressible child breaks through and reaches to one of the distinctions which society allots to its outlaws. So Mr. Lindsay's imagination and non-conformity may have been fostered and quickened by an unbending though well-meaning family and community.

Nicholas Vachel Lindsay was born in Springfield, Illinois, November 10, 1879. There were ominous signs at the very outset.

His mother noted them, and we wonder how she interpreted them. At birth the child was long, thin, with the face of an old man, and he looked as if he had the experience and wisdom of age. He had over his face what is called a "prophet's veil!" He was named for his father, Vachel T. Lindsay; his grandfather, Nicholas Lindsay; and his great-grandfather, Vachel Lindsay.

Owing to a dangerous illness in infancy, he was not sent to school as early as he might have been. His mother taught him to read in Grimm's *Fairy Tales*. After he had learned a few words, he became so interested in the stories that he taught himself. He was fond of everything that fed his imagination, though never of war stories. He liked to lie on the floor and pore over Gustave Doré's illustrations of the *Inferno* and *Paradise Lost*. His playmates were usually girls, the friends of an older sister.

The house in which he was born, and in which he lived for some forty years, is not

BIOGRAPHICAL

without special significance.* It had been owned formerly by Mrs. C. M. Smith, a sister of Abraham Lincoln's wife, and the great President had been entertained there more than once. So the house was a treasury of legends and memories. Not many blocks away was the Lincoln Home itself, which had been converted into a sort of museum. On its walls hung the Oldroyd collection of Civil War cartoons; and they together with the vivid memories of persons who had known the President, and all the Lincoln-lore amid which the Lindsay boy grew up, furnished the background for the understanding and reverence amounting to a cult, which were to find expression later in *Abraham Lincoln Walks At Midnight*.

The Lindsay household was one of intense activity, of interest in things cultural. Dr. Lindsay and his wife were, as I have said, people of an abiding and exuberant youth. Life spared them few of its severest

*It is located at 603 South Fifth Street, Springfield, Illinois.

trials, yet they refused to grow old. Their trip to China, in their last years, is proof of this. The doctor was fond of books and particularly of the Bible. From the time his children could read until they were well on in their teens, he had them memorize daily Bible lessons. Then Mrs. Lindsay had brought back from Italy copies which she had made of the masters, and she was especially fond of those writers who, like the Brownings, sang the praises of Italian art and life. Little was said of the New England writers (though later Emerson's *Self Reliance* spoke eloquently to Mr. Lindsay); the talk was always of Europe. That first glorious year abroad—the year of the courtship—was a perennial source of reminiscence and discussion, now freshened by a rereading of "Aunt Eudora's book," now by another trip to Europe. Besides, there were Mrs. Lindsay's lectures on art and her staged colloquies which quickened the family's pulse. Their church interests were of the

BIOGRAPHICAL 15

utmost importance to them; and missionary connections kept them in touch with people scattered all over the world. The boy's imagination was reached by these far away things, and he early developed a feeling of kinship with men of various countries and races.

There were certain books, too, which affected the growing child in a singular way. He has never forgotten a little blue volume of Poe's poems which had come with the family from Kentucky and which proved to be one of his first loves. Then there was a copy of Rawlinson's *History of Egypt,* a gift from his father, in which he first met an art which has enthralled him since, Egyptian hieroglyphics. The influence of still another book is told by the poet himself and reported by a relative. "The last time I visited Springfield...... (Mr. Lindsay) showed me his copy of Stanley's *Darkest Africa,* and pointing to the decoration on the cover, a map of Africa, all black with the Congo traced in gold, he said: 'That made an indelible impression on my childish mind, which stayed with me as I grew up and finally found expression in the *Congo.*'"

By the time the boy was sent to school, his parents had already decided upon his career. The poet remembers that while his father wanted him to be a physician, his mother was determined that he should be an artist.* What happened at the time was that the six-year-old boy was sent to a preparatory class in what he calls a "breathlessly exclusive private school;" and his outstanding recollection is that he possessed a drawing-book, the cover-design of which was a reproduction in colors of Guido's *Aurora.* What others remember of him is that he asked such questions as make a teacher want to live twenty years longer if only to know what strange sort of man the boy will become. There were no other boys in the Lind-

---

*Another member of the family maintains that the parents were agreed from the outset that Vachel should take up his father's profession.

say family with whom the parents could compare Vachel, so that the peculiar quality of his mind did not attract their especial attention. Yet one of his uncles dubbed him "a very seldom child."

An amusing incident belongs to this period. One afternoon the boy came home and told his father that he had kissed a girl and that she had threatened to knock his nose off if he ever did it again. "Then what will you do?" asked the father. The boy replied: "I guess the nose will have to go."

From the third grade on young Vachel attended the public schools. He must have been an alert pupil, for he skipped the seventh grade and on two occasions won prizes for excellence in composition. He would not discuss the composition subjects with his mother lest he be influenced by some suggestion. He was determined that the thoughts should be his own. He seems to have been an amiable and sympathetic child, with positive ideas of what was right, and undaunted when roused to indignation by a wrong.

It was at the age of ten that Vachel joined the Disciples' Church, and much of his thought and talk then were of religious subjects. He was moved even to try his hand at expression in verse. His allegiance to the Campbellites, like his allegiance to the Democratic party is still vital, though he would say that now it is more "patriarchal" than active. In one of his poems he has tried to recapture his childhood admiration for the founder of the sect.

Our early and intense associations are like so many blood-ties; we may trample upon them, but we cannot deny them. To a woman who was taking the poet to task for his puritanism and urging upon him a less austere conduct he retorted: "I'm afraid you are beginning several generations too late." And a similar retort could be made to the critics who carp at the godly and puritanic in the poet's work. He cannot will them

away, he cannot be made to see why he
should. They are a part of him, though
rarely the poetic part; and it is only by a
free expression of them that he can ever
transcend them. Let us regret them if we
will, but let us not forget that sometimes
they pass out of the center of the poet's consciousness, if only temporarily, and that in
those moments the singing voice rings out
clearly.

His High School companions remember
of him after thirty years that he wrote verses
and read the *Merchant of Venice* impressively. They remember, too, that though
self-conscious and sensitive the boy tried
hard to be sociable; that his efforts in the
manual training class were grotesque, and
that in spite of an ungainly gait he could
walk a mile faster than any other boy in the
school. The gait still persists, and there is
something about the man which tells that he
could not have made a deft artisan. A trace
of this awkwardness may be discernible in

the technique of some of his drawings. To the angularity of movement the man adds an astonishing suavity of manner; and the combination makes for the charm which is so large a part of personality and which is essential to success on the platform.

But Mr. Lindsay himself has recaptured a moment of his High School days and presented it tellingly. The reader will remember that Dr. Lindsay was Southern by birth and allegiance. The names of Thomas Jefferson and Andrew Jackson were emblazoned in his sky, and their doctrines were still good enough for him. He remained a Democrat, and his son followed after him. It happened, too, that Governor John P. Altgeld—"brave as the truth"—the advocate of free-speech, had been stirring the radicals with the startlingly frank interviews which he made public; and when, in the presidential campaign of '96, Bryan came out of the West voicing the aspirations of the youngbloods and threatening the entrenched conservatives, there was a profound stir in Springfield, Illinois. Altgeld was there to receive him, and for that day at least the town belonged to the Democrats.

"We roamed, we boys from High School
With mankind,
While Springfield gleamed,
Silk-lined.
Oh, Tom Dines, and Art Fitzgerald,
And the gangs that they could get!
I can hear them yelling yet.
Helping the incantation,
Defying aristocracy,
With every bridle gone,
Ridding the world of the low down mean,
Bidding the eagles of the West fly on,
Bidding the eagles of the West fly on,
We were bully, wild and wooly,
Never yet curried below the knees.
We saw flowers in the air,
Fair as the Pleiades, bright as Orion,
—Hopes of all mankind,
Made rare, resistless, thrice refined.

Oh, we bucks from every Springfield ward!
Colts of democracy—
Yet time-winds out of Chaos from the star-
fields of the Lord.

The long parade rolled on. I stood by my
best girl.
She was a cool young citizen, with wise and
laughing eyes.
With my necktie by my ear, I was stepping
on my dear,
But she kept like a pattern, without a shaken
curl."

It was in the fall of 1897 that Mr. Lindsay matriculated at Hiram College; and there he spent the next three years. Why the choice of a small obscure college?* It will be clear, if we remember that Hiram College had been founded by Disciples, still maintained its traditions, and that the Lindsays were staunch Disciples. The boy seems

*In 1900 the population of Hiram, including townsfolk, students, and faculty numbered about four hundred.

to have been an indifferent student—which may mean simply that his teachers and fellow-students found him hard to catalogue. He did not fit into the usual molds. In those days Hiram was famous for its oratorical contests, and the boy in whose family there had been preachers and missionaries for generations, the boy who was heir to the flamboyant oratory of his Kentucky ancestors took an active but, alas, inglorious part in them. He worked tirelessly and with pleasure on the illustrations for the student annuals, and this was perhaps the one thing he did well.

From very childhood the boy had been taught that he must do the things which he found hard; but with experience and growth he began to doubt the wisdom of the Spartan-like maxim; and from doubt he passed into open rebellion. Much of the curriculum had grown intolerably irksome; college did not seem to be the place for him. Why not change the old maxim, and instead of doing the things he found hard and disliked, why not try what he liked and found easy? And what could he do? He could draw; and draw he would! So without finishing his college course, and in spite of protests from home, he closed the doors of Hiram College behind him and set off for the Chicago Art Institute. A momentous decision; and while I shall not try to number Mr. Lindsay's significant adventures, I may say that he was now entering upon one of them. An intelligent and refractory boy's deliberate choice of a career is bound to have a distinct meaning.

The clash of wills between parent and child, especially on so vital a question as choice of a career for the child, is often pathetic and always interesting. If the child persists and ultimately attains eminence in his chosen field, the onlooker, who has come upon the scene too late for the battle, who cannot therefore sense the perspective and sees only the victor in the immediate foreground, is likely to lavish upon him much teary pity and to consider the parent stupidly short-sighted and tyrannical. Yet what the dutiful parent most desires for his offspring is a career as far removed as possible from the poor house and the penitentiary, a career which will bring the greatest comfort and the least pain. This being as it is, what sane parent will encourage his son away from what is assured, to so doubtful a thing as art, particularly when the child has given no overwhelming proof of disconcerting artability? It may be true that an inglorious Milton is occasionally lost for want of parental encouragement; and it may be no less true that many a potential dry-goods salesman never comes into his own because of the groundless ambitions of foolish parents. And need we be Philistine to suspect that a good workman—poet or salesman—is worth more to society than a bad one? We hear much sentimental nonsense about the superior worth of poets (and other intellectual workers); but when society grows old, and, like the individual, looks back over its life to appraise it, it may find that poets have yielded it no more and no less than anybody else.

The Chicago period lasted from 1900 to 1904, and although it seems to have been lonely and uneventful, it served to give the young man's life direction and to prepare him for what was to follow. A medical student with whom he roomed during the first year gives us this glimpse of him. "Our Sundays were spent in going to the Field Museum, the Art Institute or church. In the evenings Vachel practiced drawing and wrote. He wrote without effort and would read aloud what he had written to get the sound of it. He spent much time in rewriting and polishing his work. During the winter he sent one of his poems to a well-known literary critic of the day. We waited anxiously for an answer, and when it came it was not especially encouraging. Vachel expressed the opinion that poetry had followed beaten paths so long that something new was needed. He had an idea that perhaps he could establish a new era in literature." Here is the reformer already and he need not surprise us, for he is inherent in Mr. Lindsay's makeup, is an inevitable family legacy, one of which he will never be rid. He is at one with what the poet likes to call his spirit of adventure.

"I left the Chicago Art Institute at the end of four years," he writes, "because I wanted to study under Chase who was one of the oracles of the time. One of my great discoveries was Robert Henri who was the brilliant young teacher in the Chase school at that time." So the transition from Chicago; and on and off, for the next four years (1904-1908), the art-student was in New York. His first year was spent in study at the Chase school where he advanced as far as the life class and won the special notice of his teachers with the originality of his designs.

Seen in retrospect, the New York period remains one of the most picturesque of Mr. Lindsay's career. It is varied and many-colored, though drawing and verse-making sing through it like a dominant. Visits to the exhibits and galleries are frequent, and the Metropolitan Museum becomes a daily classroom. And there are friendships rich and ardent, fired with the idealism of struggling and undaunted youth, friendships which remain articulate through the years.

For three winters (1905-1908) Mr. Lindsay lectured to art classes for the West Side Young Men's Christian Association. In need, the young art-student sought employment of the Y. M. C. A. secretary. When asked what he could do, he replied that he could handle an art-class if one could be organized. It was agreed that he should have a class provided he could corral one, but he should receive no pay until he had proved that he could earn it. A class was soon organized, and so rapidly and enthusiastically did it grow that the teacher was able, after a week or two, to demand wages. He was accorded the munificent salary of $10 a week! "He would accept money from home," writes a friend, "only when driven by necessity, as his parents had little or no sympathy with his artistic and literary life at that time. I believe that it was in this Y. M. C. A. course that he found himself possessed of that personal magnetism and ability to hold an audience that has been such an asset to his popular success."

It was from New York that Mr. Lindsay set out for his first tramping tour in the spring of 1906. Having spent his last cent on a one-way steamer ticket, he left the boat at Jacksonville, Florida, and started his walk northward. There was war at home when his family learned that he was intending to tramp it. He would be called a tramp and the family disgraced forever. He must accept money and ride. But this, he proclaimed loftily, he would not do; and he kept his word. With the hospitable folk who gave him a meal or a night's lodging he would leave copies of verses which he carried along—*The Tree of Laughing Bells*. This tour is inimitably recorded in the first part of *A Handy Guide For Beggars,* while the latter part of the book records a similar expedition undertaken in the spring of 1908, with New York as base once more, but with New Jersey and Pennsylvania as objective. It was to allure the prodigal home from his first tramping excursion, that, in the summer of 1906, his parents invited him to accompany them abroad. There in the galleries of western Europe—England, Holland, Belgium, and France—he added to his art-lore and astonished his family with all that American Museums had taught him.

The story of the art-student's New York days is best told by the friends who remember it vividly and who helped to make those days the picturesque thing they were. "When I went to New York in the fall of 1904," writes one, "I found Vachel sitting on a brass-bound, round-top trunk in a typical hall bedroom. It was a snappy cold day; there was no heat in the room; he had his overcoat on, the collar turned up, and was writing, writing, writing. I secured a new room for him in another boarding-house. As the Muse was with him, he was very tractable, and I led him around like a captive animal by an imaginary thong.

"Vachel's idea of New York at that time was that it was a place to be converted to the love of poetry. During the day he either wrote or called upon the editors with his poems. In the evenings, during a period of some months, I recall his going from shop to shop, along dismal 8th, 9th, and 10th Avenues, trying to interest little-shop men in his poems. He had nothing to sell to them, nor did he wish to buy anything; so he must have been an enigma from their point of view. He read his verses where he found a willing ear and then passed on to another shop.

"One day I met Richard Watson Gilder, when he was editor of the *Century Magazine*. I said to him: 'Mr. Gilder, I understand that you have seen some of the writings of my friend, Vachel Lindsay.' The eye of the literary patriarch brightened and he said with animation: 'Oh, yes! I know Mr. Lindsay's work. He has a touch of genius. We should expect great things of him.'"

As the poet thinks back on his experiences with the editors of those days, he remembers something like this. He would make the rounds of the editorial offices, and in each the procedure would be about the same. He would be told that what was wanted was originality. Then he would open his folder and exhibit drawings and poems. "But all this is too original," the editor would exclaim; and the young artist would gather up his pack and pass on to the next office.

The friend last quoted goes on: "One of the interesting things that Vachel did during his stay in New York was to conduct an evening class in art for the West Side Y. M. C. A. Every Friday evening during the winters, he would take his brood up to the Metropolitan Museum and spend two hours in going from picture to picture, telling what he thought about the work itself and what he knew about the artist—his life-struggle and ambitions. His handful of students grew often into a crowd of hundreds, for many were attracted by Vachel's interesting talk and joined the throng or else came week after week on Friday nights as uninvited students, so interested were they in his personality and methods.

"Vachel was always ready for fun when he wasn't in the writing mood. He tried hard to be a good mixer, but often not successfully. At one time a considerable crowd of us lived together in a West Fifty-Sixth

Street boarding-house. About eleven o'clock every night we would go down, six or eight strong, to a cafe and have our beer and pretzels. We generally had the same waiter. As he took our order he would solemnly ask Vachel, 'What will you have?' And Vachel, with equal solemnity, would ask if he had sarsaparilla. The waiter was a foreigner, and I doubt if he ever had any idea of that famous sarsaparilla drink of fresh-water towns. Vachel would finally take ginger ale, which, I believe, he didn't care for at all; but it was less disagreeable to him than beer apparently."

Mr. Lindsay remembers his Y. M. C. A. class with affection and gratitude. He likes to tell of the class's devotion. On one occasion, in a snow-storm, he hesitated to go to the Museum thinking that none of his students would venture out in such weather. What was his surprise, on getting there, to find them waiting for him at the door!

Another friend says: "He was, as an art-student, a victim of his intense individuality, being constitutionally incapable of enjoying the life of the average student, or running with the 'bunch.' Very few, if any, of his art-student companions had any inkling of his value or purpose, although everyone liked him personally, in spite of his essential aloofness and puritanical standards. I do not mean by 'puritanical' anything more than his innate decency and distaste for vulgarity in any form."

His friends are unanimous in declaring that in matters of conduct he was entirely tolerant of the seeming lapses of others, however rigid he might be with himself. He did not set himself above others or his conduct above theirs; nor did it require any special virtue on his part to refrain from what he had been taught to look upon as licentious pleasures. There was no restraint, for these pleasures did not appeal to him, did not seem to him to be pleasurable.

Still another friend writes: "He was a most delightful friend of my early days in New York City. His force of character and thought singled him out from the majority. The first time that I met him, he had just risen from a nap taken near a window on the pane of which a snail was crawling. This had inspired him to make a drawing of the snail's dream, and perhaps he wrote a poem about it as well."*

And this from a girl friend of those days. "He knew the greater part of Milton, Poe, and Swinburne, and he would recite them in his chanting voice gloriously. It is one of my greatest joys to have heard him thus, often.

"A quixotic knight-errant, he continually delighted me with his dear foolishness and unworldiness. Coming on a visit with his shoes through on the ground in snowy weather, he gently put the money for the new

*See page 209, *Collected Poems, The Song Of The Sturdy Snails*.

shoes in the charity-box of a Catholic church —though he was a Protestant—as a little tribute of gratitude for the happy time we had had.

"He would bring his one lone orange, the only dessert his boarding-house supplied, or a peppermint stick such as a child buys."

So those days were filled with friendships, with study, with the material hardships and spiritual compensations which the struggling art-student finds in a great metropolis. Of the highest importance to Mr. Lindsay's development was his study of the Metropolitan Museum. It gave him a perspective of man's achievement in art from time immemorial to the present; and seeing what men had done in the past, he surmised the future. He began to dream of America redeemed; of the raw, industrial, and commercial land as finding her soul in beauty; and of the new localism which would make of his own home-town the center of the culture-to-be. The Museum became a Mecca to which he returned year after year with a deeper understanding of its meaning, with increased reverence. It was a shrine in which he found graven men's aspirations, their faith in the sanctity of life, their hope. It was a source of perennial inspiration. And in his statement that he has trod its echoing corridors alone for eighteen years there is pathos and a certain commentary on our civilization.

For the boy from the small mid-western city, who had been reared, in a dense atmosphere of religious and puritanic traditions, who had been destined by his family to the practical career of medicine, the New York days were a genuine adventure. They settled once and for all the direction of his future. His life would be given to art; and to sustain him he had not only the bent which years of study had given him, but also the sound and dauntless faith that society was as much in need of art as of bread, and that he could never give his full measure of service except in ways artistic.

The five years that follow (1908-1913) are among the most difficult of Mr. Lindsay's career, and at times he must have been profoundly disheartened. He refused to accept the stupid complacency of his village (as he likes to call it) and sink himself in it. His dreams of the new localism and the gospel of beauty were taking definite shape and Springfield must be made over in accordance with them. Self-sufficient communities even more than self-sufficient individuals are impatient of reformers, and Springfield was no exception to the rule. On the contrary, it asserted the rule energetically and stood ready to fight the issue to a finish.

To his fellow-townsmen, Mr. Lindsay was an absurd and impossible crank if not a downright lunatic. If he could write verses or draw, then why did he not make verses and drawings that would sell, that could be "syndicated like crackers and cheese?" Or if his art-work had no commercial value, then why not find an "honest to goodness" job and earn a decent living? To his family, too, he was a failure and a disappointment. So far as they could see his eight years as an art-student had little or no meaning; and their patience was being sorely tried by this prodigal who refused to grow up and who, after having turned his back on substantial realities, was dallying with fairies. An earnest and highly respectable family had the best of rights to expect a son to stand on his own feet at thirty. Moreover, the mutterings of neighbors were irritating to people who esteemed respect. So the clouds hung low while the crusader tried bravely to go on. At one time, when very much discouraged, he yielded to the insistent demands that he "go to work." He hired himself out for the hardest kind of work he could find; hauling coal in a wheelbarrow to the boilers of one of the municipal plants. But writing verses and sketching fairies is not a good novitiate for hauling

BIOGRAPHICAL 41

coal, and after two weeks of it the crusader's back was so seriously menaced that he had to give up his job.

Difficult years indeed, and brimful of varied activities. Our adventurer took part in organizing and maintaining debate and literary discussion. He worked tirelessly for the civic improvement of his town, helping to put into office commissioners who stood for a better Springfield. And how much, we wonder, of what Springfield has done since then, does it owe to the impetus which he gave?

For a season he made speeches on Sundays on behalf of the Anti Saloon League in the country churches of central Illinois. What hope could there be for the new localism and the gospel of beauty as long as the main square of the agricultural hamlets were sordid and ugly with saloons?

A series of lectures delivered in the fall of 1908, under the auspices of the Young Men's Christian Association, was a plea for the foreign element in our population. Instead of making policemen of the Irish, money-grabbers of the Jews, coal-miners of the Poles, fruit-vendors of the Italians—why not develop in each of these groups its particular genius? If they had contributed to European civilization, why not let them contribute to ours instead of enslaving them to our industrialism? "Springfield is full of hustlers for reform. If they make us as good as Decatur and as big as Chicago, we shall still not be unique. But the Italians can teach us how to make Springfield as rare as little Florence, and still a business city; the Greeks can remind us that little Athens proved moral aspirations not inconsistent with a noble city life for her boys.

"All cities in America are much alike. Why not make Springfield different?"

Need we be told how this new localism appealed to the crusaders' hearers? Springfield was good enough for them, and if there were cranks who did not approve, they could leave. Moreover, all this silly talk of putting foreigners on a footing with native sons was nothing short of anarchy and ought to be stopped. No telling how far it might go if the Niggers and Dagoes and Polacks were not shown their proper place and kept there. So Springfield muttered and her mutterings grew louder and louder. To her the crusader for the new localism was a dangerous loafer.

Not only undaunted, but determined to be heard, Mr. Lindsay launched in the summer of 1909 his series of *War Bulletins*. These bulletins, like the earlier tramping expeditions, were an act of spiritual warfare. The man could no longer endure the stupid indifference of his fellow-citizens. He would carry the war into their very camp, he would speak out his truth at all costs. The *Bulletins* were indeed belligerent. They struck from the shoulder and with a clarity that must have carried conviction. And although there have been occasional truces in this war of artist against the conservative industrialism of his native town, the final armistice is yet to be.

We hear of a series of lectures on Ruskin, delivered in 1911, which does not seem to have been "well received," as the local press might say. It was for these lectures that some of the speaker's fellow-townsmen wanted him, and perhaps more than metaphorically speaking, burned at the stake or sent to jail. Since 1908 the battle had been fairly incessant, and the crusader was beginning to feel the need of reinforcements. In the past, tramping and begging had been a source of spiritual healing and inspiration; the crusader would beg again. So in the late spring of 1912 he set out from Springfield and tramped to New Mexico. The trip was fruitful in many ways. The new localism expanded into the gospel of beauty for America. New poems were conceived and written. The letters home, descriptive of the trip, formed the basis for a book later;

and at the end of the journey Mr. Lindsay wrote the poem—*General William Booth Enters Into Heaven*—which won him recognition as a poet of unmistakable power. With the publication of the poem and later of the *Booth* volume (1913), he became a national figure. His public life from that year to this is told, for the most part in the record of his recital tours and publications. Of his adventures with books I shall speak later; of some of his other adventures I should at least make mention here.

I have already spoken of the trip he made to England, in the late summer of 1920, accompanied by his mother. This was undertaken with the hope that it would be beneficial to his mother's health and in response to the invitation of English men of letters whom he had met in America. The following summer he tramped with Mr. Stephen Graham over the Rockies of Montana, as told in Mr. Graham's *Tramping With A*

Poet In The Rockies,* and in the poet's *Going-To-The-Sun*. He has made several tours of the United States "singing" and discussing his poems. For the better part of two academic years (spring of 1923 and the 1923-24 school-year) he conducted classes at Gulf Park College, Mississippi. Since then he has left his life-long home in Springfield and gone to Spokane, where in the spring of 1925 he was married to Miss Elizabeth Conner. "Engaged one day and married the next," the newspapers reported; from which we may deduce that it would be hardly wise to predict what an adventurer of Mr. Lindsay's stride may do next.

*Many readers of this book have thought the verses included were Mr. Lindsay's. They are Mr. Graham's.

CHAPTER II

The Prose Books

1

If to write sincerely and convincingly of America, one must know not only her people but likewise her varied physical aspects, then who can be better prepared than Mr. Lindsay? And who else has had the courage to see her afoot? He has studied her people without neglecting their material background. East, west, plain, and mountain, all have echoed to his tramping feet, yielded nourishment to his questing heart, sharpened his sight, given vigor and color and the tang of Americanism to his writings, and made possible such inimitable books as the first two we are about to discuss.

A Handy Guide For Beggars is a record of the tramping journeys undertaken from

New York in the spring of 1906 and the spring of 1908; and although it was not published in book-form (1916) until after the *Adventures* (1914) it records earlier experiences. So the sequence followed in my discussion is that of the events recorded rather than of the publication of the books.

The first expedition led the poet northward through Georgia, North Carolina, Tennessee, and Kentucky; while the second took him through New Jersey and Pennsylvania westward to Hiram, Ohio.

"There are one hundred new poets in the villages of the land. This *Handy Guide* is dedicated first of all to *them*." It is dedicated also to all the outcasts and day-dreamers who flaunt their pride and rebellion like banners. Yet, no sympathetic reader will believe that the book is not dedicated to him personally. It takes us all out of home, shop, office, classroom, pulpit, and tilled fields, and allures us down the road where we saunter along at one with our guide, who,

The Prose Books

in turn, is at one with his beloved St. Francis in the presence of the beneficent sun. The book is one of spiritual regeneration through contact with sincere and primal things. It is a book for business-men, politicians, preachers in comfortable pulpits, professors of literature, ladies, "new poets," and no end of others. We all need a bath in the Falls of Tallulah; all need to ride in a caboose with the man with apple-green eyes; all need a night's lodging in the house of the loom. There business-men will learn how to make less money, which is what they need to know; politicians how to serve their constituents; comfortable preachers how to exhort the soil with a plough six days a week instead of unregenerate mortals, with guarded words, one day a week; professors to appraise men and life instead of dusty books; ladies to take on the ways of women; "new poets" to whistle behind a yoke of oxen; and the "no end of others" to contribute what they can to the holy order of the brotherhood of man.

What I mean is that no one can read this book without questioning much of the sophistication with which we hedge ourselves in so smugly and uncomfortably. We share in Mr. Lindsay's reverence for the simple and profound virtues, the patriarchal living which he found among the good folk who gave him food and shelter; and if we have goodness of heart and sanity, we shall wish that we, too, had the courage to turn beggar.

The book is not a sermon, it is a holiday. It is a call away from the iron wheels of commercial and industrial centers to the leisurely gait of the open road and the kindly hearts of an elemental people. Mr. Lindsay has turned tramp because his soul has become clogged with factory smoke and needs an airing. It cannot function properly, cannot serve mankind efficiently until it is cleansed and made whole again. And who would not be proud to follow at times the path which "wanders back through history till it encounters Tramp Columbus, Tramp Dante, Tramp St. Francis, Tramp Buddha, and the rest of our masters?"

But remember that this tramping is not a vocation; merely an experiment. And when this experiment will have been tried, life will still hold out a variety of others. When Thoreau had lived his two years or so at Walden Pond, he knew what such an experiment had proven and could prove; but he wanted to try others. He stood ready to return to that mode of living if he saw fit, but he was under no obligations to it. So, too, with Mr. Lindsay. He took to the road because people said that if he stayed rhymer and artist, he would be a beggar and die in the poorhouse. His most intimate friends prophesied it incessantly for years, after nourishing themselves on business-men's clubs and office-supply advertisements. Therefore, in no sentimental mood, but actually to try out this beggary, and deliberately calling himself a beggar to the end of his days, he took to the road, and tried, as it were, the poorhouse at its worst, that he might get used to it. Such is his own explanation, and almost in his own words, of his tramping experiment; and he adds: "People are far too sentimental about my begging days and talk as though they were over. I stand ready to beg tomorrow and to the end of the chapter, rather than write a line I do not want to write, recite for a routine audience, or go through any parrot or ape performances, even if I am parroting and aping what I myself happened to be twenty-four hours ago."*

No one will forget the people he has met along the road of the *Handy Guide*: Napoleon the Third (a travelling salesman who wore moustaches like the emperor's), the Gnome, the Old Lady at the top of the hill, Lady Iron-heels, Gretchen-Cecelia, and a host of others. No attempt has been made

Village Magazine, fourth imprint, page 116.

The Prose Books 53

to create them. They are part of the living text, although they may be robed in a glamor lent them by a grateful heart; and he who has read the book has met and knows them.

The humor of the book is infectious and no less ingratiating than the characters. We shall not soon forget the delights of the chapter on the Man in the City of Collars; for like the collar-salesman we, too, have succumbed to the author's Ancient Mariner eye and his mesmeric rhymes.

Much of Mr. Lindsay's humor lies in his seemingly artless satire. On one occasion he spends a night at a mission in the "richest village in New Jersey."* A series of incidents, during which the poet is treated as if he were an escaped convict, culminates in an argument with the "attendant" as to whether the poet must wear to bed pajamas which have been worn by most of the tramps

---

*The deep secret of this town's identity is revealed on page 143 of the *Village Magazine*, fourth imprint.

in America with never a wash-day interim. Poet-like he gets the worst of the argument. As he slips into the pajamas he repeats to himself: "Blessed are the meek, for they shall inherit the earth." The lights go out, he kicks off the pajamas and sleeps. He awakes at midnight, reflects on these matters and this time murmurs: "I was naked, and ye clothed me."

However, his satire is sometimes far from being "seemingly artless;" and there may be a surprise in the "Sermon on the Mount" for critics who see our poet as a godly hymn-singer or a chanting Y. M. C. A. secretary. We are still in the mission which clothed him when he was naked, and an "unmitigated" clergyman appears to help the mission in its "problem."

"I presume this clergyman imagined Christ wore a white tie and was on a salary promptly paid by some of our oldest families. But I share with the followers of St. Francis the vision of Christ as a man of the open road, improvident as the sparrow. I share with the followers of Tolstoi the opinion that when Christ proclaimed those uncomfortable social doctrines, he meant what he said."

The mention of St. Francis is not accidental. He is the patron saint of the *Handy Guide;* and he who knows the *Laudi* will find more than one echo of the praises of the beneficent sun in Mr. Lindsay's writings. And in the spiritual exaltation which renounces the comfortable paths of the world for the humble one which leads to the brotherhood of men, is there not a certain kinship between the lovable saint and the advocate of the gospel of beauty?

2

There is an inevitable resemblance between the *Adventures While Preaching The Gospel of Beauty* (1914) and the *Handy Guide.* Both are accounts of tramping expeditions; both are planned in about the same way, and the *Adventures* seem like a continuation of the *Handy Guide*. The former is, for the most part, a series of letters written home from the changing scene of action; the latter is more like the amplification of diary notes. Then, too, there is more continuity in the narrative of the *Adventures*. Once more there is need for spiritual recuperation, since the period (1908-12) in which the crusader has been trying to convert the home-town to his way of thinking has been strenuous and exhausting. Besides, the road holds out another promise. Mr. Lindsay's hope for democracy in America is rooted in his faith in America made beautiful. For the time being, at least, the machine-made and machine-maintained cities are sterile ground. No seed of beauty can take root here. But in the hamlets, the agricultural villages, where are found the patriarchal families, the "blacksmith aristocracy," there will be found also the soil which awaits the seed. So with a pack full of rhymes, and posters that expound the gospel of beauty, this Johnny Appleseed tramps across the farmlands of Missouri and Kansas. Again he exchanges his rhymes for bread (or whatever substitute is offered him) and nails his posters to fences where the farmers will be sure to see them. Even the irate farmer who discharges him because his strength gives out in the midst of harvesting cannot escape the rhymes which the poet hands him as he takes his leave.

As early as the *Village Magazine* (1910) the gospel of beauty had been pretty clearly defined. The crusader now proposed to sow his doctrine broadcast through the middle west. The talented children of every village were to be given an art education, one that would voice the democratic aspirations of the nation. Then as painters, sculptors, architects, dancers, craftsmen, and poets, they would return to their native villages where each would expound and develop his particular art. And no less earnest than their faith in art was to be their faith in the righteousness of God. It was politic and inevitable that the new gospel should have the religious tenet; politic, because it would not antagonize the simple folk for whom it was destined; inevitable, because it is a basic and large element in Mr. Lindsay's creed.

The posters which the adventurer carried were reproductions of drawings for the *Village Improvement Parade;** and conspicuous among the rhymes to be traded for bread were *The Proud Farmer, The Illinois Village,* and *The Building of Springfield.* These three poems gave the "best brief expression of my gospel."

The sceptic will shrug his shoulders, laugh, and may go so far as to doubt the adventurer's sanity or offer him a job with the railroad section-gang. But why should we agree with the sceptic? The flight of words is incalculable, and beauty strikes unexpectedly and subtly. And the seeds of the

*See the *Village Magazine,* pages 14-19.

gospel of beauty which the adventurer has sown will as surely be fertile as were the appleseeds of Johnny Appleseed generations ago.

Now it so happened that as the adventurer fared westward a new and vast horizon loomed up before him—wheat-harvesting in Kansas; and the book which begins as an exposition of the gospel of beauty swells into the passionate song of the great harvest. The apostle finds a larger and more eloquent exposition of the gospel of beauty than he himself had dreamed, identifies himself with it, and when, after further wanderings, he swings homeward again he is carrying a weightier pack than that with which he had started. His faith in the agricultural village, in the rural population, in true democracy for America, has increased a hundredfold. The never-ending expanse of the Kansas wheatfields has entered into his soul. America will listen to the gospel of beauty and she will be redeemed. This is the voice of the wheatfields, the song of the harvest.

Mr. Lindsay is genuinely interested in men. He observes them shrewdly, and understands them with rare insight and sympathy. In his suggestions for social reform he is always sound, and doubtless because he prefers to give rather than to extort. He was one of the first to point out that in our petting and grooming of engines, in the surrender of our individuality to machinery, lay the problem of much of our social unrest. And in stating his economic position he sets forth truths not acceptable to certain classes but bound to prevail sooner or later. "I have thought of a new way of stating my economic position. I belong to one of the leisure classes, that of the rhymers. In order to belong to any leisure class, one must be a thief or a beggar. On the whole I prefer to be a beggar, and, before each meal, receive from toiling man new permission to extend my holiday. The great business of

The Prose Books 61

that world that looms above the workshop and the furrow is to take things from people by some sort of taxation or tariff or special privilege. But I want to exercise my covetousness only in a retail way, open and above board, and when I take bread from a man's table I want to ask him for that particular piece of bread as politely as I can."

As of the *Handy Guide,* St. Francis is the patron saint of the *Adventures.* He is invoked repeatedly; and his benignity and compassion inform the book throughout. Here is the very quintessence of Franciscan humility and charity. The adventurer is speaking of an old couple, keepers of a little shelter which houses a stationary engine, and where he seeks a night's lodging. ".... seldom are keepers of engine-stables as unfortunate as these. The best they can get from the world is cruel laughter. Yet this woman, crippled in brain, her soul only half alive, this dull man, crippled in body, had God's gift of the liberal heart. If they are supremely absurd, so are all of us. We must include ourselves in the farce. These two, tottering through the dimness and vexation of our queer world, were willing the stranger should lean upon them. I say they had the good gift of the liberal heart. One thing was theirs to divide. That was a roof. They gave me my third and they helped me to hide from the rain. In the name of St. Francis I laid me down. May that saint of all saints be with them, and with all the gentle and innocent and weary and broken."

The incidents are always picturesque and fascinating, often humorous. What more flattering to a knight of the road than to look so much like a Gypsy as to be mistaken for one by the Gypsies themselves! And memorable are the stop at the section-gang's shanty, and the adventurer's request to the men who are throwing through the open door perfectly good sandwiches and pieces of pie, that they wait until he get out there to catch them; and the occasion on which the schoolmaster "gets the poet's goat" for doubting his authorship of the poems he has been reading; and the harvest hand who puts by his pornographic rhymes in favor of the chorus from *Atalanta In Calydon*.

Then, too, the student of Mr. Lindsay's poems will find in the *Adventures* the sources, so to speak, of the *Santa Fé Trail*. The old Negro who explains that a certain bird is the Rachel Jane; the automobiles with their horns and pennants; the fast trains; the handcars; the good folk who stare at the crank drawings; the strawberries by the roadside; the grasshoppers which eat holes in a man's shirt; all are there. And the account of the broncho that would not be broken of prancing is not only masterly prose, but a finer piece of verbal expression than the poem—good though it be—on the same subject.

3

All of Mr. Lindsay's books are signed unmistakably with his personality. Now over this personality there preside two genii, one good and one evil. They rarely exert their influence separately; and often, too often, the evil genius predominates. This does not imply that the influence of the evil genius is wholly baneful and that of the good genius wholly sound. On the contrary, the evil genius is sometimes salt to what might otherwise be insipid or ballast to what might be so airy as to escape this world of ours altogether. The good genius presides over the artist and brings him visions of bubble queens, owl queens, bodiless boats, maps of the universe, and breathes into his ear the whisperings of the moon, the song of exotic birds, the restlessness of the dead; while the evil genius keeps a strong hand on the reformer, harangues him in a loud and raucous voice to the effect that the world can be saved from sordidness by democracy, and that though America is not now the best possible of democracies she can become such, if she will make an aristocracy of the work-ing-classes, wash away her unpuritanic sins, go to church on Sundays, and accept the gospel of beauty.

The promptings of these genii are evident in most of Mr. Lindsay's work, but nowhere are they more sharply contrasted than in the books discussed in this chapter. The first two, written during the ascendency of the good genius, are books of adventure, fascinating in what they narrate and in the manner of narration; the later two, with too much of the evil genius about them, are theses which often demand more sympathy with the writer's ideas than they are capable of evoking and which lack the inspiration of what we commonly regard as creative art. So in discussing them we may be fairer to the author and clearer to our reader if we restate as best we can the essential ideas.

In the *Art Of The Moving Picture* Mr. Lindsay stands before the film, tilts his head, half-shuts an eye, and tells us what he thinks is wrong with the film and what we should do for it. In other words, this book is not a scientific treatise but an artist's impressions by way of criticism, and his constructive suggestions. We are warned that this is "*not* a book of tips on how to make quick money off the films, but a book exhorting people to lose money on them for a hundred years till they evolve into something worthy of the Blacksmith Aristocracy of one hundred years hence."* This is precisely the attitude that we have learned to expect of Mr. Lindsay. He is applying the gospel of beauty to the large and groping industry of the moving pictures. He finds the moving picture to be potentially the most powerful agent in the cause of democracy that we have yet developed. It reaches farther than magazine or newspaper, has a quicker and more irresistible appeal, and for these reasons should be made to serve the people rather than the mercenary individual.

Village Magazine, fourth imprint, page 112.

It is already thirteen years since Mr. Lindsay's book first appeared; and while the pictures have developed, they have not gone very far in the direction that he indicated. People who read books on moving pictures are, for the most part, those who want tips on how to make quick and easy money. Art is long; so, too, is the gospel of beauty. Most of us have seen the informational value of the screen; we have still to realize its possibilities in civic and cultural directions. Yet, for those who dream of Americanization through art, what more powerful, what farther-reaching medium than the moving picture? Only the large centers have art museums, but the humblest and dingiest hamlets have picture theaters and can see the same pictures that are to be seen in the metropolis.

Mr. Lindsay divides moving pictures into three groups—action pictures, intimate pictures, and splendor pictures. Between these and the arts he finds subtle correspondences.

He sees in the action pictures sculpture-in-motion, in the intimate pictures painting-in-motion, and in the splendor pictures architecture-in-motion. Arbitrary categories at times, but with room enough for many a fine vista not only in what has already been done but also, and more especially, in what may still be done. No film need be made up entirely of sculpture-in-motion projections; but perhaps we may think of it as a sculpture-in-motion film if the great bulk of its projections is of the sculpture-in-motion type. And so with the other two categories.

The action picture is one which is set in the open and which is of the cowboy-rounding-up-his-herd type. The principal characters become the racing man and the animals; hence the sculpture-in-motion category. The intimate pictures, which deal with the quieter, more restrained moods, take an interior for setting; and in the shifting space relations of the objects and persons concerned, we are reminded of such masterpieces as those of Rembrandt. Hence the painting-in-motion category. The setting for the splendor pictures, as for the action pictures, is the out-of-doors; but in splendor pictures the vast background of mountains and forests or of buildings becomes animate. It broods over and dictates, as it were, the moods of persons in the foreground. Hence architecture-in-motion.

Yet these categories, however interesting in themselves, are of secondary importance. The great central fact is that Mr. Lindsay has discovered and established a correspondence between the photoplay and the fine arts. He has thrown open a "charm'd magic casement" through which photoplay makers will sooner or later behold marvellous things. Then we shall see the work, not of ex-vaudeville managers, but of artists who know and utilize in their productions the world's great art treasures. Then we shall have motion pictures which will recall this or that great painter, this or that school; motion pictures which will suggest now sculpture in wood, now in bronze; motion pictures which will awaken in us the mood of the acropolis or the mediaeval cathedral. Such pictures are not only possible, they are inevitable.

The book is full of sound practical suggestions. We have seen that a beautiful moving picture must keep a certain space relation between the various persons and objects that appear; so, too, must there be a subtle relation in the movements of these same persons and things. They should not all move to the same tempo; there must be variety to prevent mechanical effects.

As the makers of beautiful photoplays will be men acquainted with and profiting by the art of the world, so the artists, in turn, will find the photoplay an invaluable museum and studio. There they will see and be able to study individuals and groups, in motion or at rest, in ways impossible of access heretofore.

With each passing year we are realizing more fully that the stage and the moving picture are not to be confused, that they are distinct arts. The one is verbal, the other pictorial; and as long as we remain a "word-civilization," as Mr. Lindsay calls us, the stage will hold its own. Ibsen cannot be done on the screen nor the burning of Troy on the stage. However, there are still too many photoplays which offer us words when we want pictures; and, as our author points out, it is fatal and disillusioning when a film ends with a paragraph instead of a picture. The photoplay should be so constructed that each new scene is more beautiful than the last, and the climax the most beautiful of all. The whole mechanism should work like a kaleidoscope which halts when some exquisite harmony has been achieved, then moves on displacing the bright bits of glass only to attain still more exquisite relations. The constant progression of the film should be towards a tranfiguration of actors and accessories.

We have seen that the art museum could be made an invaluable ally by the photoplay maker. Another source of training and experimentation would be the puppet-show. And not only can the puppet-actors be of value, but the puppet-accessories as well. By experimenting with these, as the architect and landscape-gardner experiment with models, the photoplay maker can add enormously to his resources. Then there are hieroglyphics to be utilized; and there is no more suggestive chapter in the book than that devoted to hieroglyphics. Its application is clear enough. The photoplay is picture writing; the hieroglyphics of the Egyptians were picture writing. Might not the study of the ancient art be helpful to the modern? In the photoplay, actors tend to become types, consequently hieroglyphics; while hieroglyphics and mechanism tend to become human. That is, everything on the screen is a symbol charged with human significance. What else were the hieroglyphics of the Egyptians? And, as Mr. Lindsay says, the study of primitive picture writing is as apposite to photoplay making as would be the study of Hebrew to Bible interpretation.

That a social reformer should see in the picture theater a substitute for the saloon was natural but short-sighted. It was at best the expression of a hope, not the statement of a reality. The enormous amounts which our government spends in trying to enforce the eighteenth amendment are proof enough that if the saloon has gone, it is not the picture theater which has taken its place. Man has an inordinate capacity for dissipation; and to open up a new avenue is not necessarily to close an old. Moreover, if we look a little deeper, we shall see that as long as nepenthe can be reached by the obliteration of the intelligence no less effectively than in the exercise of it, the conversion of adherents of the one to the other mode of behavior is likely to be arduous.

A sounder suggestion of Mr. Lindsay's is that our makeshift orchestra be eliminated from the picture theater. The only kind of music suited to the photoplay is music especially written for it. There would be necessary, then, a real orchestra to play such music. All this would tend to make the performance more expensive and to put it out of reach of the people who need it most. The photoplay would cease to be a democratic art. Besides, while the music and orchestra might be possible in the large centers, they would be out of the question in small ones. Better neither the music nor the orchestra which we now have, for they only cheapen the photoplay. As a substitute for the orchestra Mr. Lindsay would have the audience encouraged to talk and to discuss the picture before them; not in a way to prove a disturbance, but as becomes an orderly and democratic gathering.

In his criticism of the new art, as in so much that he has done, Mr. Lindsay is pioneer as well as adventurer; and the analysis which he made of the moving picture several years ago is still the basis for photoplay criticism. One need only glance at the periodicals to realize how much the contemporary critiques are indebted to the *Art Of The Moving Picture*.

This, like the others of Mr. Lindsay's books, is only another chapter in the exposition of the gospel of beauty. It is through beauty that America is to be redeemed, is to be made a true democracy; and since the moving picture is the most widespread of all the mediums of beauty, its opportunities and obligations are correspondingly large. Mr. Lindsay knows that the film can be made a disseminator of news and even of scientific information; but he knows also that scientific experimentation *per se* will never redeem America, never make it democratic. Our one hope lies in spiritual expansion, and the only way to spiritual life winds among the foothills of beauty. "Beauty is not directly pious, but does more civilizing in its proper hour than many sermons or laws."

4

It is possible to pick up the *Adventurers* or the *Handy Guide* and to enjoy, and, for the most part, understand them without ever having heard of their author. Not so the *Golden Book Of Springfield* (1920). To read it understandingly one must have a thorough acquaintance with all that Mr. Lindsay has written. Still that will not suffice; and even to the careful and sympathetic reader the book is bound to prove baffling, perhaps altogether disappointing. Yet, it cannot be overlooked, for it contains much that the author holds dear; and an unbroken line runs from the earliest of his writings straight through the *Golden Book*. Not because of its mysticism is it difficult reading, but because it is badly written. It is sorely in need of a preface, one in which the writer will explain how, after the book had been planned and partly written, it was broken to bits, rewritten and enlarged in an attempt to make it more entertaining to the "average reader." All this in conformity with bad, commercially-minded advice. The result has been disastrous. Instead of making the book more readable, the added matter has virtually ruined it. It is now diffuse and often trivial. As originally planned, it was to be a sort of Village Magazine of Springfield, a group of essays, a book no more consecutive than the Koran; and all that has been introduced to give it a sort of consecutiveness is extraneous and misleading.

The *Golden Book* is Mr. Lindsay's dream of his beloved hometown made over after his own heart's desire—Springfield of a century hence made regenerate according to the dictates of the gospel of beauty. "What doctrines are not absurd to the soul that refuses to receive them?" asks the *Golden Book;* and those who cannot or will not understand, have seen in Mr. Lindsay's doctrine, nothing but puritanism. The real doctrine, however, is one of priestcraft. The poet's mother had been a spiritual leader and had nurtured dreams of a unified church. Alexander Campbell, the great theologian of the Disciples, had dreamed similar things. So the spiritual leadership, the priestcraft of this book was in Mr. Lindsay's blood and training. Symbolic of this leadership is the cathedral, and it is around the cathedral that the Springfield of the poet's dreams gravitates. A mediaeval town is the Springfield of 2018, with its cathedral and city walls. The wall may be more or less spectral, a matter of local color; but no one who knows the poet will doubt the solidity of the cathedral structure. Nothing would delight him more than to know a huge Gothic cathedral in the midst of his city, a cathedral reminiscent of Notre Dame of Paris in its architecture, and of all the great creeds of the world in its spiritual aspects. And this cathedral, center and dispenser of the brotherhood of man, would be the great healing and guiding presence in the heart of the city. Here is a book the "heroine" of which is a cathedral.

Not only will Springfield of 2018 have wall and cathedral; it will have beautiful public places, a university, Sunset and Truth Towers, and a select population. The blacksmith aristocracy will have come into its own, and a man will be as proud of being a blacksmith as we are proud today of belonging to one of the oldest families or of being worth millions. Wealth will be considered a crime. It will be possible to differ from one's neighbor in creed, but all men will be united in civic allegiance. And since municipal government is a kind of nest-building, women, the home-builders, will take an active and large part.

As the cathedral is to be above all creed distinctions, so in the citizenship of the new Springfield there are to be no race prejudices. Every race will be welcome and every man will help round out the soul of the town by bringing it his race's special gift. The Irish element will contribute one thing, the German another thing, the Italian still another, and Springfield will be the richer and prouder for them all.

The same sound political ideas that we find elsewhere in Mr. Lindsay's work reappear here. There are to be no privileged classes, no castes. How admirably does the Japanese gentleman sound the note of warning! "Do not go on perpetually climbing into office because you can recount military history, as many of our Samurai have done, drowning out the man or woman who wants to speak of matters thirty years ahead and plan such a thing as your Fair or University. No war ushers in the perfect state. The great wars are not all fought with the sword. To speak in the Christian phrase, remember that every yesterday is but a box of costly spikenard to be broken on the feet of Holy Tomorrow. Though you fight ten wars, let yesterday be your enemy. Otherwise you fight but as the nations that died before Confucius and Mencius." And we should know by now that Mr. Lindsay is not one to be overburdened by yesterdays and the need for consistency. His business is with today's forecast of tomorrow.

The plan of the Prognosticators' Club was an altogether happy idea, for it allowed the writer to project himself in many ways. Springfield of the future as twelve persons see it, is Springfield as seen through twelve different windows. What they reveal is like so many prophecies. Readers have thought they recognized various persons in the members of the club, but such a conjecture is groundless and unimportant. What is significant is that in certain aspects of several of the personages we may recognize traits of Mr. Lindsay himself. When Sparrow Short exclaims: "Live like the sparrow. Be yourself completely. Utter your soul regardless of cost," we are listening to the war-cry with which the poet has had to fortify his soul through many years. And the mottoes of the same personage remind us of those to be found inscribed on the posters of the *Village Improvement Parade*. There is one more memorable thing which we must associate with the artist Sparrow Short. He is one of those rare teachers—the only true teachers—whose object is to promote the diversity of their pupils.

When Boone speaks, it is again the poet we hear. "In a whirlwind world, independent languor becomes a virtue, and meditation a finer art than nervousness." But it is as St. Friend the bread-giver that I like him best; and St. Friend, by the way, is the only one of the several characters in the book who takes on anything like distinct individuality. For the most part, these characters remain undifferentiated save for their names. St. Friend is as lovable as his favorite saint, Johnny Appleseed, and most of the stirring passages in the book are put in his mouth. "Will the millenial future be a tin and wire world, an electrical experiment station, and no more?" Or again: "The best wings are spirit wings, however we fly with them. It is better to be like Shelley than to have the glory of Langley and Wilbur and Orville Wright." It is St. Friend, too, who champions freedom, "yet his kind of freedom goes to prayer, of its own choice, with no theological or creed fences, to what he calls 'the blessed company of all faithful people.' "

We have often been reminded of Thoreau in reading Mr. Lindsay's prose; and the *Golden Book* sends us back in thought to *Walden*. Both books look towards the millenium; but while Thoreau would attain it in the triumph of the individual, Mr. Lindsay would reach it in the triumph of the masses. Thoreau wants simplicity; Mr. Lindsay, the art-student, would have splendor,

Incongruous as is the *Golden Book,* it contains many an exquisite paragraph, much sound idealism. It is not a pleasurable book, nor yet a negligible one. For Mr. Lindsay's prose at its best, we must return to the *Handy Guide,* and the *Adventures.* These two books, like the best of his poems, are unique. They are better constructed, sustained at a higher level, than any of his books of poems; and in years to come they will be as fresh and readable as they are today. In originality, in native flavor and charm, they must rank with the best prose books that Americans have written.

CHAPTER III

The Poems

1

When, in 1913, Mr. Lindsay entered the regular channels of the book trade, he was not making his initial appearance between covers. During the preceding six or eight years he had had printed several booklets of verses of which the most ambitious was *The Tramp's Excuse*,* issued in the summer of 1909. Yet, none of these booklets had won him more than a local bow; and it was not until Miss Harriet Monroe had called attention to the *Booth* poem and Mr. Kennerley had published the volume in which *Booth* serves as title-poem that Mr. Lindsay got a national hearing.

*Reproduced in part in the *Village Magazine,* fourth imprint.

The *Booth* volume is fairly indicative of Mr. Lindsay's talent. His later volumes have been a development of much that was manifest in the first. It is unevenness itself, contains some of his best and some of his worst, and represents the man rather than the poet alone. And this latter is a point which we must keep before us in trying to appraise Mr. Lindsay's work. His books are an autobiography; and he insists that it be complete and honest. The core of his writings, what he calls his ideas, is very often his reformer's program; so he is likely to disappoint readers who insist on what they label "pure poetry." Nevertheless, it is always fascinating to see how a man so laden with a moralizing pack, can set it down now and then, stand upon it and thence take wing.

In this first book the poet sings the promise and joy of the open road, gets badly mired in an anti-vice crusade, succeeds in making inspired verses of the tenets of the Anti-Saloon League, fires a broadside of vituperation at corrupt politicians, preaches the gospel of beauty and the brotherhood of man, amuses the children with moon-songs and dancing potatoes, and holds up for our emulation his chosen heroes. In much of this work there is more novelty of matter than of treatment. There is very little departure from the older conventions of prosody, and too often there is puerile imitation of other poets. But all this leaves out of consideration the title-poem itself and such other poems as the airy, little *Queen of Bubbles,* the profoundly touching and deep-toned elegy for Altgeld, and *On The Building Of Springfield* with the marble calm of its Attic structure. There is a distinct note of Americanism in this last-named poem as there is in *Booth;* but in *Booth* there is also an originality of idiom and handling not to be found elsewhere in the book. The poet has found himself at last, and it is from the van of General Booth's brigade that he will advance to his finest achievement.

Rather odd that one of the first of the poems in which Mr. Lindsay voices his Americanism should have to do with an Englishman and an institution founded in England. Yet the Salvation Army and its band of hard-worked enthusiasts parading city streets by night had become so firmly rooted in America as to make up an authentic part of our daily life. And how authentic the setting! Suddenly from an alley or cross-street emerges the little group to the beating of the bass-drum; and the tambourines, the shrill and discordant voices, the strains of the well-known revival hymn, the march round the court-house square, the halt by the curb-stone, all these are things which we have heard and seen. No preliminary description; the band breaks in upon us and the scene unrolls exactly as we have often witnessed it. Nor is it a common thing to find in a short poem such telling images of sight, sound, and movement.

Let us remember that while the scene is so realistic as to have taken place in our city streets, it actually occurs in Heaven. The streets are those of Paradise; the actors are the poor mortals who, though rejected by humanity, are acceptable to Christ; and the passersby who stop to look on are God's saints. Literally, the poem is the apotheosis of the Salvation Army; symbolically, it is the apotheosis of all derelicts and the glorification of the most compelling aspect of Christianity, the humanity of Christ. The appeal to the imagination of Christendom through the Christian conception of Paradise, the verisimilitude of the scene, the humanity of Jesus, the fact that the poem voices the best of human aspirations and in a very human way, make for its profound spirituality.

No less significant than the appearance of *Booth* was the poet's oral presentation of it; and the two combined make up the outstanding adventure, the turning-point in Mr.

Lindsay's career as a man of letters. The descendant of Kentucky and Virginia orators, the boy who had struggled earnestly but without distinction in the oratorical contests at Hiram came suddenly into his own. He found himself applauded as reader and entertainer; and it was not long before the poet who had been reading conventional verses in a conventional way to small groups was pacing the platform of crowded auditoriums and thundering what he called the Higher Vaudeville. At a time when our poetry was at a very low ebb, and when a few shrewd workers were endeavoring to infuse young blood into it, Mr. Lindsay hit upon subject-matter and mode of treatment which seemed racily American. Moreover, in his method of interpretation he was making still another innovation; he was trying to restore the "primitive singing of poetry." So with the swelling of the tide, to which he himself gave no small impetus, he rose to a position of recognized eminence. The new condition was an opportunity and a menace. It won the poet a hearing, but threatened to destroy him. Neither he nor his public has ever realized fully that it was his oratory, his stage presence, rather more than his poetry which was being applauded; and even if he had realized it, he would have been left with little choice. To maintain and enlarge upon what he had already achieved he must go on as he had started. Moreover, his ideal of a poetry which would be democratic, would appeal to large numbers, and his personal endowment of orator, evangelist, and showman pointed in the one direction, the direction of public entertainment. And now that his particular aptitude, the thing for which he had sacrificed everything else, had become articulate, would he voice or silence it? He could choose but to voice it; and we shall see, as we examine his writings, that if he has often abused it, he has shown likewise the splendor of its possibilities.

2

The *Congo* volume (1914) remains one of Mr. Lindsay's best. It contains, to be sure, some indifferent work, but far less than did the first book. This is due in part to the fact that the second book includes fewer poems which date from the art-student and tramping days, but even more to the prodigious growth which the poet had made since the writing of *Booth*.

The ideas which give unity to Mr. Lindsay's work—even though they often detract from its aesthetic value—dominate here as elsewhere. Here again is the gospel of beauty, here the voice in the wilderness crying out against vice and sordidness, dreaming a Utopia, groping and pleading for some unifying and guiding principle for humanity. And the voice that is raised against warfare is now strident with condemnation, now soft with persuasive pity.

Mr. Lindsay is not much given to overemphasis of his ego; but when he does yield

—as in his amatory verses and in those poems in which he feels that his idealism makes an outcast of him—the note of self-pity is not too perceptible. And for this we thank him; for of weaknesses which make men intolerable, self-pity is the least pardonable. His platform of social reform may be indigestible to his muse; but it cannot be always and wholly bad if it saves him from superficial and maudlin introspection. The best of his love-poems are informed with the pathos of broken wings, the pathos of a child's reaching for the unattainable.

The moon-poems and other poems for children, like those we met in the *Booth* volume, may not reveal one of the larger aspects of Mr. Lindsay's talent; but they cannot be passed over in silence. He has done nothing more delightful and more fanciful; and here he comes as near to escaping from the reformer as ever he can. Less sophisticated than Mr. de la Mare's poems of childhood, these of our poet's are more nearly akin to the Stevensonian verses in which all the playthings come alive. In them the imaginative child brings intimately into his own world physically remote and intangible phenomena, and makes a toy of the moon or a banshee of a potato onto which burnt matches have been grafted for arms and legs.

The *Congo* and *the Santa Fé Trail,* which are the life of this volume, are certainly the offspring of *Booth* and could not have preceded it. Henceforth Mr. Lindsay's major poems will be descriptive and will adhere pretty closely to the principles of contrast established in *Booth*: loud and soft, light and dark, slow and fast.

The *Congo* is the best known and the most popular of Mr. Lindsay's poems. He has read it from the platform actually thousands of times, and has sometimes been impatient of the public which is forever demanding it. But this is only half of his complaint; the other half has to do with the public's understanding of the poem. The reformer would have us see one thing, and we choose to see another. If we examine the poem, we shall see that the third and last part attempts to depict the Negro as shriven of his superstition and converted to Christianity. However, the intended spiritual message is completely lost on most of us. Savage colors and gestures still flash before our eyes and the tom-tom deafens us to any softer sounds. The fault is not wholly ours. The very structure of the poem makes for the loss of the reformer's message. The first two parts, which depict the Negro's savagery and high spirits, far outweigh the regenerate third part. Besides, the repetition of the mumbo-jumbo cry at the end of the poem, even though it be but an echo, only serves to heighten the unforgetable power of the witch-doctors instead of dispelling it. It may be, too, that the poem fails of spiritual conviction because we cannot identify our own experience sufficiently with that of the people described. So the final appeal is sensuous, as indeed it ought to be.

In the back of the poet's mind at the time of composition were the Springfield race riot, his story the *Golden Faced People*,* which is based on that disturbance, and perhaps the remembrance of certain pages of Stanley's *Darkest Africa,* a book which he had read in childhood with the greatest enthusiasm. The poem seizes upon the Negro's outstanding characteristics and presents them in a dazzling and memorable riot of sound, motion, and color.

That Negroes themselves should not be more sympathetic with Mr. Lindsay's efforts to interpret their race is perhaps the best possible proof that he has done it well. What the Negro in America wants is to forget his racial traits and to have his white neighbor forget them. All of which may be excellent sociologically, and no one desires it more sincerely than does the poet himself.

*Reprinted in the *Village Magazine,* fourth imprint, p. 136.

But it is absolutely apart from the question. What the poet attempts is to portray the Negro of today, not the problematical creature of some dim future who, having lost racial color and traits, will be no Negro at all.*

The popular song, the vaudeville performance, the moving picture, all of these have entered into Mr. Lindsay's art. Pictorially his poems are often what he advocates for the moving picture—a series of tableaux. So it is with the *Santa Fé Trail*. He has returned to certain details which had been recorded in the *Adventures,* and his imagination has transfigured them. His vocal interpretation of the poem is a memorable thing, but somewhat ironic and therefore misleading. Although he plies the loud pedal vigorously, it is really the soft interludes upon which he would insist, and which his violent contrasts seek to bring out. However, it is fairly clear that what most of us

*See *Village Magazine,* fourth imprint, pages 134-135.

carry away is the tooting of the horns and
the noise of the trains. These, we think,
are the voice of our great industrial America,
and we hail as a representative American the
man who has put them into his verses. We
fail to see that the Rachel Jane is the hero
and that his song is the voice of beauty calling through the din of our iron-bound land.
Time and again, through the hot dusty day,
that small sweet voice is drowned out; but
in the calm of evening, when everything calls
us to rest and meditation, the bird-song rises
once more and this time dominates the scene.
It is the bird-song which the poet has heard
and followed and wished us to hear, not the
horns and the iron wheels. It is we who
have intruded into his dream with our noise,
while he has been trying to silence us with
the pipings of a little bird. The song of
the Rachel Jane is the poet's hope that America may still be redeemed. After she has had
her day of bustle and clangor, she may in the
evening, grown weary and wiser, be willing

to listen to the soothing songs of her Rachel Janes. In spiritual power the *Santa Fé Trail* takes rank with *Booth*. It sweeps us with the cleansing wind of wide spaces, brings us the healing of the beneficent sun, and makes us akin to the grass and stars.

3

There is a close sequence and gradation from *Booth,* on through the *Congo* and the *Santa Fé Trail,* to the *Chinese Nightingale;* from the poem in which Mr. Lindsay found himself, through those in which he perfected his medium, to that one in which he achieved his utmost. The overworked tone-contrast, which makes the *Congo* and the *Santa Fé Trail* deafening and distracting at times, is far less noticeable in the *Nightingale*. In fact, the *Nightingale* comes nearer being wholly a song for the "soft pipes" than any other of the poet's longer compositions.

How admirably he succeeds in beguiling us back to the great days of China's golden age! A Chinese laundry in San Francisco, night, the smell of burning joss-sticks—and we have the basis of fact whence his imagination takes wing. Then out of the smoke of the burning incense rise lady and nightingale, and together with the Joss they evoke the picture and music which the laundryman had known, ages before, in a former incarnation. And to make us more keenly aware of the spell cast over us, the poet breaks in suddenly with a lurid glimpse of the San Francisco back-alleys. Once more the sharp contrast without which Mr. Lindsay could hardly be himself. Then the spell again, and it overpowers us more completely because of the break. Nothing could be more like a magnificent dream which overtakes us in a moment of drowsiness, and its opiate-like effect is a necessary part of the poetic mood. The wisps of song which the nightingale intersperses throughout the poem are exquisite, and its inimitable finale remains the poet's finest lyric utterance.

In its combination of imaginative power, sustained effort, and necessary technique, the poem is unique among Mr. Lindsay's. It excels in splendor as *Booth* did in simplicity; and while the latter may seem, because of its Christian setting, more intimately spiritual to the occidental mind, the former's appeal may be no less profound and more nearly universal—the appeal of sheer beauty. Here, as seldom, didacticism and the rest of Mr. Lindsay's annoying *isms* have fallen away. The poet is swept along irresistibly and voices purely and adequately his peculiar gift of song. Here is the height to which the Higher Vaudeville has led; and while the path may be difficult, it is clearly not a bad one. The *Nightingale,* unlike so many others of Mr. Lindsay's poems, does not need his ornate delivery; it can rise readily from the printed page and soar on its own wings.

Now for the reverse of the medal. This third collection of Mr. Lindsay's poems,

The Chinese Nightingale And Other Poems (1917), contains his finest poem and an almost unpardonable heap of trashy verses. Following the title-poem comes page after page of prosy didacticism and sheer drivel. We are grateful indeed for the occasional respites. The finely evocative and disciplined imagination of the *Nightingale* has gone, and in its place we have, as in the *Tiger Tree,* a riotous undisciplined imagination, which beats about in a meaningless jungle of words. Aristotle's probable impossible and possible improbable get sadly tangled and so mutilated that only the impossible and improbable emerge.

No one can ever accuse Mr. Lindsay of being so condensed as to be obscure. His sins are in the opposite direction. His preacher and orator ancestors have the annoying habit of resurrecting, and he of mistaking the resurrection for an inspiration. The result is often dire. These evil genii may induce him to mount a soap-box in the pub-

lic square and harangue an invisible crowd
or to write an epitaph fifty lines long! One
cannot deny one's forebears, and Mr. Lindsay's cling to him for life and death. Yet,
out of his weakness sometimes comes his
strength; and to the tense religious atmosphere in which he was nurtured he owes many
a happy inspiration. No small part of the
stuff of his imagination is of the kind we find
in Bible stories and hymnals; and the inspiration for the finely elegiac *How I
Walked Alone In The Jungles Of Heaven*
seems to spring from a sort of homesickness
for the white-portaled Paradise of childhood.
Moreover, the Negro sermons appeal and
convince because they evoke admirably that
Otherworld which so stirs the childish and
primitive in us.

For a poet to voice our Americanism, it
will not suffice that he dot his verses with the
names of Washington and Lincoln, Chicago
and San Francisco; he must express, because
it is his, something which is racially ours.

Mr. Lindsay feels that the Indian has left his imprint (perhaps in spite of us) on our civilization; and he takes Pocahontas as symbol of that vestige of her race. Where once resilient grass was soft under her moccasined feet, are now our city streets, streets which seem to have forgotten her, yet cannot deny her; and because they cannot deny her they make authentic the vision of the poet who, looking upon them and remembering, sees

"Flames coming up from the ground."

No less authentic is his evocation of the primitive life which surged across our plains not many generations ago, shadowy Indians on all manner of strange mounts racing westward in the deep night, carrying shadowy torches, painted, hideous, yelping their blood-curdling "a-la-la, a-la-la," and followed by shadowy buffaloes which thunder westward, they too, with their great lolling tongues and heaving sides, and disappear as do the Indians in the night and the past. And in spite of its "night before Christmas" sing-song and setting, the *Ghost Of The Buffaloes* leaves a vivid impression. If for nothing else, it would be memorable for the magical little flute-song of the wind in the chimney, a song which is of the poet's best, and which is comparable with the songs of the Chinese nightingale and the Rachel Jane.

In endeavoring to establish a closer relation between poet and public, to rouse a democratic art-consciousness, in short, to develop a nationalistic poetry, Mr. Lindsay has utilized suggestions which he has gleaned from certain forms of expression in which there is group participation. He remembers that the ancients wrote poems for choral chanting and dancing; he knows that in the church services there is mass participation; he has observed the communal spirit in children's games; and he has seen the vaudeville actor take the audience into his confidence. These suggestions he embodies in the Higher Vaudeville—which I shall discuss later —and in what he calls the Poem Games.

These latter are intended to be danced and chanted. In some, like the *Potatoes' Dance*, the emphasis will be on the dancing; while in others, like *King Solomon,* the emphasis will be on the choral chanting. That the poem games, as Mr. Lindsay conceives them, have possibilities, and legitimate ones, he himself has shown; but they lie in the game rather than in the poem direction. In the poems to be danced, the words yield the foreground to the dancing figures; while in the poems to be chanted they are dominated by an extraneous and superimposed tune.

These poem games are not unlike the masques which certain communities have produced. The essential difference is that Mr. Lindsay's form of group expression is simpler and can be effected more easily. And quite apart from my feeling that while the poem games may furnish good parlor entertainment they are hardly likely to set in motion or quicken a nationalistic poetic pulse, the *Potatoes' Dance* is a delightful poem for children, and *King Solomon* just such a vision of Paradise as we fancy the Negro's Heaven to be.

4

With the growth of interest in poetry during the past decade or so, there has come a corresponding and insistent demand that we break with the English tradition—that is, that we write of things American and for Americans. And some critics have gone so far as to claim that we have a lingo of our own, sufficiently unlike English as to be distinguishable, and to demand that our poets use it. But the great expanse of our country, the diversity of its parts, has shown us how difficult, if not utterly impossible it would be for any artist to compass the whole; so we ask that he speak for his particular locality, confident that if he does, he will have contributed something recognizably American. It is as if we compared America with a large family, the members of which would be her poets. In the utterance of each we should find the individual and something more, not uniquely his, which he would have in common with the others, his family resemblance, his Americanism; and if we examined the collective utterance of several or of all members we might find most of the family traits, the essential Americanism of our generation.

Mr. Lindsay has always advocated Americanism and localism; and while his earliest work showed no marked tendency towards an essentially American idiom, it is interesting to note how with each volume he has got more and more of our lingo into his speech, until in his fourth collection he characterizes his poems as being "rhymes in the American language." There is much of this "American language," however, which is pure jargon; and instead of adding localism, Americanism or anything else of value, it only detracts. One would need a special glossary with which to wade through it.

Still, taken as a whole, the *Golden Whales* volume (1920) ranks with the *Congo* volume as one of the poet's best. It contains much excellent work, though nothing which reaches the high level of the *Chinese Nightingale*. The initial piece in the book has little to recommend it as poetry, but is good as satire; and satire, surely, has its own right to be. As Daudet in the *Tartarin* books, shows the effect of the bright sun on the Southern Frenchman, so Mr. Lindsay shows the effect of a kindred sun on the Californian. In both countries the sun goes to one's head and intensifies the imagination. However, the Frenchman, though he see mirage, is not vitiated by it; he retains his geniality, remains a "cheerful liar." Not so the proud native son of California. Not only does he see double, but in the self-sufficiency which sees in California God's chosen country, and in the native sons God's chosen people, the Californian becomes intolerant and intolerable. But this is only one of the scores which the poet has to settle with the Golden Gate. Another, and doubtless more important has to do with the moving picture industry. The man who saw in the moving picture the best possible medium for the dissemination of the gospel of beauty has a right to be at outs with the state which has commercialized and vitiated our newest art. California has acquired the Midas gift and her childish excitement is still at its height. Not even her darling daughter—the moving picture—is safe from the accursed touch; nor is it clear just when California will realize that the gift is a curse. Hardly a wonder that the good St. Francis—lover of the poor and humble—should stand aghast on visiting the site which bears his name!

We are accustomed to characterize as "fish tale" a highly colored and improbable story. When the coloring becomes too vivid, the story too bold, we call it a "whopper;" and there may be only a short step from a "whopper" to the golden whales which the Californian sees. However that may be, Mr. Lindsay has succeeded very well, and with more humor than flail-blows, in ridiculing the gold-struck and perfervid imagination wherein

"Goshawfuls are Burbanked with the grizzly bears."

The poet makes a new and happy departure in *John L. Sullivan* and *Bryan*. We may perhaps call them chronicles, since both are re-creations of moments in the life of America. *John L. Sullivan* is more gentle in tone than in its implications; for it is not very flattering to our national pride to be shown that back in the listless eighties we sang "East side, west side" and held our breath as we awaited reports of the Sullivan-Kilraine fight. And we wonder how flattering to our national pride it would be to compare the listless eighties with the nineteen-twenties!

One need never have been enthusiastic about Bryan's mentality to like the *Bryan* poem cordially. A poet lives all his poems after a fashion; but the fact that the poet has lived this one in a material sense adds to its vividness and authenticity. It is a reliable chronicle of the temper of the times, of the issues, the passions, the personalities of Bryan's first presidential campaign. Politically speaking, Bryan was to be reckoned with in those days; and the enthusiasms which he, and the issues he stood for, roused in his adherents, the stir which they caused in the rival camp, live again in Mr. Lindsay's poem. It is more than a chronicle; it is an impassioned and dynamic drama. In the first acts we have the exposition of the issues and the conflict which results; then Hanna rallying the conservative forces; then the climax—the defeat of Bryan; and lastly the fine, contemplative stanzas of the epilogue. The poet handles his subject with consummate skill throughout, sustaining us in the early parts with action, and at the close with meditation and poetry. Even in the earlier, the more oratorical parts, we are kept aware

The Poems

of his essentially aesthetic attitude by the recurrence of the fine verse

"Bidding the eagles of the west fly on."
And the poem is memorable for a score of other things: the glamor of Bryan's oratory; the concise and graphic episodes; and the epithets with which the poet pillories persons and things—"Bull-dog Hanna," "lean rat Platt," "victory of the letterfiles," "Mark Hanna's McKinley, His slave, his echo, his suit of clothes."

As a crusader for peace, Mr. Lindsay is attracted by the races which, like the Chinese, prefer meditation to aggressiveness. In *Shantung* he shows us how China, said to be crumbling thousands of years ago, has outlived the great western empires. And he prophesies that it will still be standing when many others will have crumbled away. The meek will have inherited the earth. Memorable and haunting is the beautiful and varying refrain which serves musically as the dominant to which the ear likes to return, and logically as the link which connects the present and future generations of men with those which have already receded into the sombre past.

In theme this poem suggests the *Chinese Nightingale,* and it resembles it in lyrical quality. An essential difference, however, is that while the latter has an American setting—a laundry in San Francisco—the former is foreign in setting as in theme. This may seem to be a superficial difference; yet *Shantung* is the only one of Mr. Lindsay's major poems which is not in a sense American. Even the *Nightingale* draws a certain vitality from the contrast between its theme (a dream of Old China) and its setting (an American Chinatown). And in spite of the fact that *Shantung* is well written and of large import, it seems to lack the salt of Americanism which we find abundantly in most of the poet's work and which serves to leaven it.

The Poems

We must not think that the chronology of the publication of Mr. Lindsay's poems is dependent upon that of their composition. In his latest books are found poems which were written years before the publication of his first volume. The *Last Song Of Lucifer,* which first appears in the *Golden Whales* volume, was written in 1899 when the poet was a student at Hiram. In one of his prefaces* he says of this composition that it may serve as a key to such rhythms as he understands; and it is only as a basis for his prosody that it can interest us now. We shall come back to it presently, but for the moment let us consider what we have observed of Mr. Lindsay's rhythms.

In much of his work, notably the shorter poems, he has followed conventional patterns and often his pattern is determined by that of a revival hymn or popular song, of which he wants to utilize the tune. In the remainder of his work the principle of his rhy-

Collected Poems, 1925, page 5.

thms is simple enough. First, let us remember that his verse is composed to be read aloud, and primarily by himself. It means, then, that his own voice with its possibilities and limitations is to be a determining factor. He retains enough of the conventional prosody —rhythm, assonance, and rhyme—to give his work the semblance of what is commonly accepted as verse, and, according to the particular demands of the composition, adds what elements are necessary to the desired end. And these elements are gleaned from his varied literary, oratorical, song and hymn-singing training. The total effect is a gait varying back and forth between the irregular cadences of common speech and the more regular ones of oratory and song.

Mr. Lindsay had observed how vaudeville actors, with a seemingly informal presentation—they sang, spoke, acted, danced, as mood or role or expediency dictated—established a certain intimacy with their audience, and this appealed to him as democratic if not as art. Something like it, then, would perhaps afford the best possible medium for his democratic gospel of beauty. Moreover, his own platform manner—in many ways he is no mean showman—was not wholly unlike that of the vaudeville performer; and with these or similar things in mind he called his method of presentation the Higher Vaudeville.

Now for the connection between the Higher Vaudeville and *Lucifer*. The latter is quite unoriginal and smacks strongly of Poe from whom the younger poet has taken, among other things, the device which he uses so extensively and variously of repeating a sound, a phrase or a verse. Its rhythms are essentially conventional; and if we follow Mr. Lindsay's suggestion that they mark his starting point, and if we compare them with the rhythms of *Bryan* or the *Santa Fé Trail,* we shall see that among such singing rhythms as those of *Lucifer* he has interpolated the rhythms of oratory and simple speech. And it is in this combination —of Poe and Mark Twain, as it were—that he achieves the Higher Vaudeville, and gives us something which is unmistakably American and original.

In the preface just referred to, Mr. Lindsay waxes hot over the critics who assume that all he writes is "loose oratory or even jazz." He admits, however reluctantly, that he has written "jazz poetry," though he claims never to have used the word "jazz" except in irony. What the critics in question have done is merely to ticket the poet and his work with a convenient and not altogether ill-fitting label. And the poet himself should neither scorn nor disparage what is admittedly "jazz poetry;" for who will say that it may not be a valuable contribution to American letters? Whether poetry or not, it is perhaps an excellent reflection of the aesthetic ideals of an unimaginative and industrial age.

Our constant drifting from coast to coast has deprived us of roots; and where there are no attachments, there is little emotional life. Ours is an age of bewilderment. We have let go the old props before we have found new ones; and we seek to fill the void with a staggering and ceaseless physical agitation. It is this condition that is reflected in "jazz music" and in Mr. Lindsay's "jazz poetry."

Now the "jazz poetry" is only the Higher Vaudeville carried to one of its extremes; the higher reduced to the lower vaudeville. At one end of the scale stands the *Chinese Nightingale;* at the other, stand things like the *Apple Blossom Snow Blues.* Knowing the songs of the Negroes and the popular imitations of them, the poet has slipped their syncopated rhythms into his Higher Vaudeville and has adapted them to his poems of Negro life as well as to others. Readers who will not admit of humor in poetry (and Mr. Lindsay's is an abundant and often two-edged humor) or of anything which does not seem to them to partake of the "high seriousness" will find no place in their lives for "jazz poetry." Yet who can read the *Apple Blossom Snow Blues,* for example, and especially the direction, "grand finale of jazz music, like the fall of a pile of dishes," without realizing that much of Mr. Lindsay's "jazz" is sheer irony? And this irony was unmistakably present in so early and so fine a poem as the *Santa Fé Trail,* as I have already pointed out. We should notice, too, that even in the "jazz poems"—*Daniel* and the *Blacksmith's Serenade*—the structure is analogous to that of the *Chinese Nightingale*. It depends on the principle of sharp contrasts, which I discussed earlier; and while this principle involves the introduction of drum, trombone, xylophone, saxophone, and the other *bones,* it makes due provision for the flute solo. And from pole to pole of the Higher Vaudeville the flute solo is the kernel of poetry for which the noisy orchestration affords a baroque and ironic setting.

5

With the publication of his *Collected Poems* (1923) Mr. Lindsay rounded out his first decade as a national figure. It is characteristic of the man that the book should be of his collected rather than his selected poems; for, as I have said, he insists on the autobiographical aspect of his writings and refuses to omit any of the chapters. In this volume he has included virtually all that had appeared in the four preceding, some recent poems, and some which had served as interludes in the prose books.

The autobiographical foreword is hastily written and lacks the charm of the best of Mr. Lindsay's prose. It does serve to clear up certain misconceptions; but too often it is trivial and its undertone is petulant and controversial. Despite its interest, its barbs and its humor, one feels as he reads it that the poet is taking himself too seriously. And how much he regards his work as autobiography is hinted at in such a statement as, "I do not expect to get ten feet from my childhood till I die."

The circus-day crowd, the election-day crowd, the Negroes, the Salvation Army, the Gypsies—Mr. Lindsay has sung them all; and if, taken as a whole, they do not represent all of America, they do set off distinctive facets of our national life. Here in the *Kallyope Yell* the poet voices the mood of the agricultural community which turns out to see the circus; and there in *Johnny Appleseed* is the throbbing life which drove our fathers across the Applachians and made possible the conquest of a continent. Then there is the Gypsy poem which may have germinated in the incident—told at the beginning of the *Adventures*—where the tramping poet is mistaken by the Gypsies for one of themselves. At any rate, it is the cry of Gypsy fiddles, heard or imagined, which kindles the poet's imagination, stirs the wanderlust in his heart, and is the poem's psychological starting-point. Always an adventurer, Mr. Lindsay gives us in this poem his first blank verse. It moves with a befittingly easy and elastic gait, and in a closely woven sequence and with bewitching sounds and colors, the untamed "proud and stiff-necked and perverse" tinkers, fortune-tellers, and horse-traders pass before us, gull us and mock at our gullibility, and dream all the while of a distant and alluring fatherland to which they hope some day to return.

It would have been better if the poet had retained only the best stanzas of the *Litany Of The Heroes** and had let them stand as individual poems, for they remain distinct and disconnected. They show no progression; one stanza merely displaces another. Some of them like those on Lincoln and

*An earlier version, entitled *God Help Us To Be Brave,* was issued privately as a pamphlet in New York in 1908. Later several stanzas appeared as individual poems in some of the poet's books.

Columbus are wholly admirable, as are verses and epithets in many of the others. But on the whole, the *Litany* lacks distinction, is not characteristic of the poet's best manner and is hortatory rather than inspired and inspiring.

The book is impressive for its youthful outlook and vitality, its breadth, its tang of Americanism, and its essential unity. Even a casual glance will reveal many and varied poems of undoubted excellence. And a poet is measurable, after all, in terms of his successes. A good part of this book could have come only from a true and original poet; and in this part Mr. Lindsay ranks with the best of his contemporaries and with those of his elders who have made a distinctive contribution to our creative literature.

CHAPTER IV

The Picture Books

1

If we glance back at the first issue of the *Village Magazine* (1910) we shall find that Mr. Lindsay was looking forward to the time when a book might enjoy a magazine's privilege of combining prose, verse, and drawings. Some of the books which he has published recently may approach his three-panelled ideal, though none comes as near to it as does the *Village Magazine** itself. Here the man finds elbow-room for his expansiveness, for bubbling over from one medium into another, and he wanders at will from prose to drawing, and from pictures to verse-writing.

*Except where some indication to the contrary is given, my discussion of the *Village Magazine* will be based on the fourth imprint.

Mr. Lindsay is sometimes a bad critic of his own work; yet he has often sensed—and sooner than anybody else—his particular protuberances and set them off with a graphic expression. It was he who dubbed himself *adventurer,* who saw the *jazz poet* in his verses, and who signed himself *designer.* His is a pictorial mind, and his drawings are essentially design. They articulate his ideas; and he tells us that when the same idea has furnished a drawing and a poem, the drawing has come first. The verses are in illustration of the drawing, and this explains why he calls them inscriptional. So the particular title which I give to this chapter of my discussion must be understood to mean: books containing pictures rather than illustrated books.

His drawings are not unlike his poems. Almost always fantastic, they are now simple, now over-ornate; now comic, now mystic; now grace itself, now woodeny and uninspired. Many of them would make effective posters, book-cover decorations, *culs-de-lampe,* pictured fairy tales; and a few might fit into our newspaper comics.

If we remember that Mr. Lindsay has been drawing continually for at least thirty years we may understand the force and charm of the best of his designs without understanding necessarily why they have escaped detection so long.

I have spoken earlier of his interest in Egyptian hieroglyphics. Art studies, and later the development of the moving picture may have quickened this interest. At any rate he saw in the picture-writing of Egypt the record of a civilization and he began to think of interpreting his own people in terms of picture-writing or, as he would say, in "United States hieroglyphics." The experiment is still in its beginnings, yet a casual glance at the picture books will reveal something of the artist's manner and direction.

Now if we approach his drawings with the prejudices of academic training we are likely to miss their significance completely; but if we will see them as he meant that we should, as hieroglyphics, we cannot fail to appreciate their truth and consequent beauty. To take an extreme example, we need only look at the drawings of the Land Horse and the Sea Horse to realize that they are picture-writing. If in the Land Horse we try to see our generally accepted horse, we pervert the artist's intention and find only a monstrosity; but if we look for what he meant that we should see—the symbol of a creature broken down by hard and promiscuous usage—we cannot fail to find and appreciate it. So, too, with the Sea Horse. The very fantasticality of the beast suggests pride that never could be humbled by bit and martingale.

Here in the *Village Magazine* is the first considerable exhibit of Mr. Lindsay's drawings; and this extraordinary publication is the cold-frame whence were taken and developed many of the seedlings which now flourish or languish in the artist's books. The few pages of prose which prepare the way for the *Golden Book* are a terser advocate than is that much diluted book, and an editorial like the one on the *Holiness Of Beauty* transcends the didactic and burns brightly. Then there is the enthusiastic tribute to Johnny Appleseed, as fine a piece of writing as any Mr. Lindsay has done. But I would stop a moment longer on the drawings. Here are village paraders, enthusiasts of the new localism, full of the aggressive spirit of youth and fired with the conviction of visionaries; while from the celestial censers which swing over the city there emanates a spirituality which is a veritable bread of the angels. Then as we turn the pages we come upon the mystical wedding of rose and lotus (far finer than the poem on the same subject); the ghoulish soul of a spider; elfin-creatures like the owl-queen; the candle-moon with its cold blue light (although these drawings are all in simple black-and-white); and the mystical Blake-like map of the universe which is so far removed from the earthliness of machine-driven America as to be virtually unintelligible to us. And if we glance at the mottoes inscribed on the banners carried in the village improvement parade, we catch still another breath of the idealism which informs this unique magazine, mottoes like:

"A hasty prosperity may be raw and absurd

A well-considered poverty may be exquisite"

and

"Without an eager public all teaching is vain."

It is almost incredible that after four imprints of the *Village Magazine* have been made and distributed gratis, it should still be so little known; for now that Mr. Lindsay has enriched it by including, among other things, his *War Bulletins,* it represents him more nearly than anything else he has done, voices his particular truth adequately, is almost all that we can know of him and almost all that we need to know.

2

The *Village Magazine* suggests what cannot be an altogether fortuitous analogy. To know Mr. Lindsay's work is to realize that all of it combined—poems, prose, drawings— makes up a sort of *United States Magazine,* a super-edition of the *Village Magazine* broad enough to compass the nation. It seeks to reveal the actual and potential soul of America as the lesser magazine seeks to reveal the soul of Springfield; and each of the artist's successive publications is as another chapter in this larger book. That the latter is not and will never be completed goes without saying; but its insistent idealism gives it unity and singleness of purpose. So Mr. Lindsay's talk of hieroglyphics is no idle day-dream, no eccentric pose. His writings and his pen-and-ink drawings are the authentic hieroglyphics with which he tells us the American story as he experiences it.

The vast panorama of the American out-of-doors has been a fruitful inspiration to him, and his tramping excursions have furnished materials for much of his best work. If we recall the *Handy Guide* and the *Adventures* and group with them the books which we are about to discuss, we shall see that together they make up a rare canticle to the sun.

There is something arbitrary in my choosing to classify as picture books, books containing poems to which I shall give special attention; but Mr. Lindsay's drawings have been so little recognized that I desired to emphasize them by devoting a separate chapter to the books in which they appear. The three books which lie immediately before us have so much in common that my approach may be more direct if I discuss them as one.

The Picture Books 133

The man who has won a hearing in one of the arts often finds it difficult to be heard in another. The public refuses to believe in his versatility, finds it easier to have a single label for him, and, if he ventures out of the first category assigned to him, will drive him back to it with cries of "each man to his last." The people who roared with laughter when Molière appeared as Sganarelle or Scapin would desert his theater when he risked a tragic role. Lamartine's fame as poet was a distinct drawback to the orator and statesman; and here and now the public does not differ much from that of another time and another country. So Mr. Lindsay, whose first public hearing was accorded to the poet, has found it difficult to convince us that he is and was first and essentially an art-student. For long years he had tried vainly to induce publishers to allow him to combine drawings and verses in his books; and when, with *Going-To-The-Sun* (1923), he succeeded at last, that step marked not only an adventure but a decisive victory.

It was in the summer of 1921 that with his friend, Mr. Stephen Graham the English writer, he made a tramping expedition in the Rockies; and although they "almost slid into eternity," they seem to have had a jolly time of it. Some months later Mr. Graham published an account of the trip;* and *Going-To-The-Sun* "is a sequel and a reply" to that account. The two books are complementary and together give a vivid and entertaining account of the journey. Mr. Graham's book was illustrated by an artist in London, who did not make the trip and had to rely on the former's verbal description for the basis of his pictures. The mountains he drew were not sufficiently steep for Mr. Lindsay; and those the latter has drawn make up for the deficiency. The difference in point of view is interesting and not alto-

Tramping With A Poet In The Rockies, D. Appleton & Co., New York, 1922,

gether unaccountable. Mr. Graham was an experienced and expert mountain-climber; and it may be that to his practiced eye the slopes did not appear as nearly perpendicular as they did to his companion. A glance at the mountains which Mr. Lindsay has drawn will suffice to convince us that he has certainly felt them. We seem to understand, too, why he lagged behind and we suspect that the sounds which reached Mr. Graham on his superior heights were sometimes reverberations of the poet's panting and not always snatches of an uninterrupted hymn-singing.

The prefatory *Elements Of Good Tea*, though carelessly written, is not without the good qualities characteristic of Mr. Lindsay's prose: seeming spontaneity, humor, gentle irony, and intimacy. The verses, we are warned, are merely incidental and serve to explain the pictures. One of the pieces, however, deserves a place as satire beside the *Golden Whales;* and that is the delightful

So Much The Worse For Boston where a Colorado mountain-cat, which has only *heard* of Boston, describes the Boston of his dreams with the "wild and wooly" vision with which Bostonians, who have only *heard* of what lies west of Boston, are accustomed to see the West. We suspect, too, that in this poem Mr. Lindsay remembers rather vividly a certain review which emanated from the high-heeled suburbs of Boston and which condescended to find some merit in his poems but which could not forgive him his supposedly middle-west origin. But it is of the drawings included in *Going-To-The-Sun* that I would speak especially.

It has often been said that there is a potential novel in every man's experience, and Mr. Lindsay maintains that there is potential drawing in the pen-stroke of our handwriting. In his own drawings he follows no rigid formula, but may take a written word and carry out the curves which the letters and his fancy suggest until he is satisfied that he has drawn the picture of which that particular word is capable. But the written word is not always the starting-point of his drawings; he sometimes begins with a mental picture. The drawings which fail to convince are those which seem most labored and least fantastic. Among the best are such hieroglyphics as his mountains. They are not scientific nor photographic representations, but the symbol, the universal truth of mountains; and if ever any symbols for mountains spelled ruggedness, steepness, height, his surely do. Besides, they are fraught with spiritual suggestiveness. Their summits are like dazzling minarets which reach heavenward.

The essential growth over the drawings of the *Village Magazine* lies in the direction of spontaneity and airiness. The *Thistlevine* might be wrought of gossamer or cloud-shreds; and figures like those of *Meditation* and the fairies which spring from the apples of Johnny Appleseed have an other worldliness which sends us back to the shadowy ladies of the Preraphaelites.

When in the summer of 1921 Mr. Lindsay was tramping through Glacier Park he little suspected that four years later he would return there with his bride for their honeymoon. But so it happened; and this honeymoon afoot in the mountains of Montana is recalled in the drawings and verses of *Going-To-The-Stars* (1926) and *The Candle In The Cabin* (1926). So these two books are like a continuation of their predecessor, and all three are to be put with the *Handy Guide* and the *Adventures* in one delightfully companionable group. While the prose books are more directly concerned with the physical aspects of things, the others seem to dwell essentially on spiritual meanings.

The press notices of the books under discussion have been all too cursory. Perhaps the reviewers had exhausted the store of smart things they had to say about Mr. Lindsay's poems, and his drawings are a novel if not wholly cryptic thing. Yet here again are mountains which only the soul can climb, flowers which grow on such mountains, and such other phenomena as only the inner eye beholds. We delight in the *Midnight Wind,* the *Flapper's Pride,* the *Mohawk Fantasy,* and *Wallpaper For The Sky;* and we wonder what could be more charming in their utter simplicity and completeness than *Coeur d'Alene,* the *Quail, The Baby,* the *Bee That Left A Smoke Trail,* the *Curling Waves,* the *Palettes And Brushes Of Autumn,* the *Musical Butterfly,* and the guttering candle of the epilogue. I cannot recall drawings done with a few sweeping lines which have pleased me as do these. And how omit others of the candles, the *Heart Boat,* and the *Little Fish?* Nor should we overlook the beautiful Egyptian hieroglyphics into which something of our artist himself has passed.

The introduction to *Going-To-The-Stars* is not uninteresting, but it lacks Mr. Lindsay's breezy spontaneity, and for reasons which will be obvious to the reader. The foreword to the other book is a terse exposition of the principle of the pen-stroke as a basis for drawing, a principle to which I have alluded earlier.

As to the poems, many of them afford plentiful evidence that the poet is still in full possession of his singing voice. Here are songs of and for America; songs which glorify her past and are full of hope for her future. Our poet is an admirer of strong men, of men who stir the imagination and sway the hearts of their fellows; and here he shows us Andrew Jackson,

"Old buffalo knee-deep in the weeds,"

a very special saint in Mr. Lindsay's calendar, trampling down the Secessionists and saving the Union with the sheer strength of his indomitable will. And the poet who is loud in his praise of the savior of the Union likes to look back at his own far-away ancestors and to sing softly of Virginia with

The Picture Books

her traditions, her great names, and her pride in her blue blood. Others have seen the beauty of the little dirge for the flower-fed buffaloes, the tone of which, by the way, sends us back to Sandburg's *Cool Tombs;* but I would call attention to the enduring hope in youth and democracy which sings through *Nancy Hanks* and the *Angel Sons,* to the large and kindly heart of *Three Hours* and *Rain,* to the radiant fancy which creates the *Celestial Trees Of Glacier Park,* and to the sprightly and infectious whimsicality of *A Curse For Saxophones.* It is noteworthy, too, that in *Andrew Jackson* and *Virginia* the poet returns to the excellent patterns which he had fashioned in the Bryan and Pocahontas poems.

There are poems in *The Candle In The Cabin* which merit particular notice. That here the personal note should appear as nowhere else in Mr. Lindsay's poems is natural enough, for these are songs of love and love's fulfillment; but it is a mellow and deep-toned note, a note which rings with independence and security and yet is tempered with the solemnity of pathos. What evocative overtones in the elegiac *Hall Of Judgment* and in verses like

> "The ten hunting dogs in my heart
> Have captured forty-six years
> In a wood that is dewy with tears!"

Poems like these bring something new into the poet's production, and we hail them as a good omen. Nor is this the only good omen. In these his latest books Mr. Lindsay forgets much of his customary haranguing, and the result is the companionable quality of which I have spoken. But the moralizing is not wholly absent. The three last stanzas of the *Parable Of Deepness* ruin what would otherwise be a complete and effective poem; and a similar criticism applies to the final stanza of *A Curse For The Saxophone*. Besides, in poems like this last-mentioned, one feels that the poet is too conscious of being on the defensive. The "jazz-poet" label still smarts like a mustard plaster.

3

Since I have already discussed the *Collected Poems,* the enlarged and so-called illustrated edition wants little more than a word of explanation. The drawings which have been inserted have been taken from the *Village Magazine,* and I need hardly add that they are not illustrations for Mr. Lindsay's poems. It is the verses which accompany them that are illustrative. Of some of these drawings we have already spoken; I shall return to two of them presently. Excepting the drawings, the most valuable addition which this book makes is the autobiographical *Adventures While Preaching Hieroglyphic Sermons.* This with its companion-piece, the *Adventures While Singing These Songs,* and the bomb-laden *What It Means To Be A Poet In America* which appeared recently in the strangest of corners,

A MAP OF THE UNIVERSE ISSUED IN 1909. THIS MAP IS ONE BEGINNING OF THE GOLDEN BOOK OF SPRINGFIELD

The Picture Books 145

will afford an excellent approach to a study and understanding of Vachel Lindsay, poet, adventurer, pen-and-ink artist, and citizen of the United States.

But to return for a moment to two of the drawings included in this edition—the *Map of the Universe* and the *Queen of Bubbles*. The latter dates back almost a quarter of a century to 1904, the former to 1909. The Map, which is of a distinctly religious inspiration, recalls the mystical visions of Blake and appeals to us for its quaint yet childlike symbolism, its cosmic sweep, its remoteness from the commonplace and its consequent spirit of idealism. The dainty and fairylike Queen of Bubbles, seated on the drift of radiant and ascending bubbles which are her chariot, clasping one knee with her hands and with her rapt face raised in contemplation of the sun-bubble, is the most delightful of the artist's pen-and-ink creations; and the composition as a whole, in charm of inspiration and technical completeness is perhaps the finest of his more elaborate drawings. To these two drawings one can return repeatedly with a sense of discovery and of renewed pleasure.

CHAPTER V

Conclusion

Conservatives have always nursed the notion that our literature was and should remain a sort of colonial appendix to English literature. Moreover, the breadth of our country, the natural diversity of its parts, its youth, the heterogeneous character of its population, have made it difficult to seize upon what was typical of the whole, to know just what Americanism of thought and expression might be. Yet, as time and circumstances broadened the breach which geographic remoteness and political independence had started, the clearer-sighted and bolder of our thinkers saw that any further attempt to dog after the English tradition would be retrogressive; and retrogression in a land of pioneers was not to be thought of. These men were willing to acknowledge and accept their English legacy, but they insisted on utilizing it for their own ends and in their own way. Increasingly they felt that they could not present something which they did not know because it was not theirs; and that *something* was the English point of view. On the other hand there was something which was theirs, which they knew, and of which they wanted to speak; and that was their own habitat and their own people. What happened then is what happens everywhere, even in countries of a lesser area and a closer-knit population. Americans began to write of their particular localities and developed the literature of New England, of the South, of the Middle West, and others. All of these have some common element which an objective observer might sense and call Americanism. Likewise each has its individual peculiarity, its localism.

Of recent writers none, perhaps, has been a more ardent advocate and a better exemplar of localism than Mr. Lindsay. He would have the artist voice first his own village, then expand until he attains to a national consciousness. His own development has gone by some such stages: poet of Springfield, poet of the Middle West, and now interpreter of America in terms of "United States hieroglyphics." That he is recognizably American is, I think, undeniable; and that he should be is natural, for he is the voice incarnate of the great masses of our people. Not that he has made or willed himself so, but that he was born to the manner and could not escape it. The family in which he was reared was the typical, God-fearing, law-abiding, respectable American family of a generation ago; and he differs from the environment in which he grew only in intensity. He is the concentrated essence of that environment. In him his community has become articulate. Moreover, his native Springfield is one of a thousand undifferentiated American towns, towns which have been syndicated from coast to coast; so when he speaks for Springfield, he is speaking for America. And readers who ask of our contemporary literature that it be a manifestation of our twentieth century democracy, the democracy of unreflecting youth —and what country is so dominated by its youth!—the democracy of brass-music, speed, nerves, popular education, and of the exploitation of everything from the soil to God, will find it, though it may fly the colors of Utopia, in Mr. Lindsay's writings. He throbs to mass effort because he is of it, and in much of his work he sublimates the emotional life of the masses.

He lacks a sustained analytical sense. What he represents is a world remade in accordance with his preconceived Utopia. Tomorrow holds more meaning for him than does today. Hence a book like his study of the moving picture is essentially a dissertation on the moving picture as he would make it, rather than a history of what the moving picture is and has been. His heroes, too, and virtually everything he touches, he refashions instead of representing. So he is rarely out of the clouds and comes near fulfilling Keats' prescription that the poet spin from within.

The best of his prose is to be found in the jaunty and informal description of personal experiences. His drawings are little known and not likely to appeal to a people which, at best, is only verbally trained; yet they are no less worthy than his prose and poetry, and all three have a common import.

It is as poet that he has been most widely accepted, and it is to his poems that I return for a parting word. We may think what we will of them, but their influence on the aesthetic thought of our generation cannot be denied. His insistence on the spoken word as the only true basis and medium of poetry may prove to be one of his most valuable contributions.

I have alluded to the imitation of older poets which we found in his earlier work;

I have spoken of his art studies and of his enthusiasm for the picture writing of the Egyptians; yet, in spite of these things, he remains a middle-west American. His writings contain no literary subjects, and he is almost wholly free of the clouds of glory which writers along the Atlantic seaboard have come trailing out of the European tradition.

He is the victim of faith in inspiration. Everything that enters his head he puts down on paper; and he lacks the self-criticism necessary to see in his inspiration nothing but a starting-point.

His genius is lyrical, and, if not oratorical, certainly verbose. It is not without significance that one of the poets who have meant most to him is Swinburne. His longer poems, even those of which the core is narrative, are rhapsodically constructed. To the lyrical impulse he adds a quaint and richly pictorial imagination, large sympathies, and a certain intellectual independence. His weakness appears in frequent triviality, in sermonizing, in diffuseness and over-emphasis. The didactic is never long away; and in so recent an utterance as the last imprint of the *Village Magazine* he urges those readers who would know his present-day *opinions* to read his new *poems*.

Since poetry is a form of communication, the poet must not hide his light. Instead of economy of expression, Mr. Lindsay practices lavishness. Words are heaped on words until the thread of the theme is broken, the unity compromised or even sacrificed. There are times when he is trying to suggest exaggerated conditions by using exaggerated expression, but he carries it too far. He is in more than danger of becoming "drunk with words."

One may have all possible talent, but it will be frittered away in trivialities unless there be some polar star to give it direction. Mr. Lindsay has the great advantage of having started out with a faith—faith in humanity—to which he has clung through thick and thin. This gives his work unity and breadth of appeal.

There has been nothing precocious in his development. The earliest of his meritorious poems were done when he was already well launched in his twenties. Intellectually he is never profound, and emotionally only rarely. He remains well within the mean of the great masses whose voice he is. Except in his very best poems he falls below many of his fellow-poets in workmanship and inspiration. In his latest, to be found in what I have called the picture books, there is a noticeable gain in concision and in the direction of a personal lyric cadence. We do not know, to be sure, what lies ahead of him, though we may feel that while a meditative poet only ripens with the years, to a rhapsodical one like Mr. Lindsay youth is necessary. Be that as it may, what he has already done is a contribution to be reckoned with;

and while he may add to it, nothing which he will do can destroy it.

There is meaning in his admiration for men like Barnum and Bryan. They, too, were voices of the great class which he now represents. His platform delivery is something of a Barnum and Bryan duet, and the America which he sees and sets before us is like a great circus with many side-shows.

His present reputation, which rests so much on his forensic powers, will not stand. To his own generation he is primarily the interpreter of his poems. When we think of the *Congo*, our ears still ring with his overemphatic presentation of it. This will not be true of another generation. The poet will be appraised ultimately from the printed page, and never can black and white make of the *Congo* what his voice and gesture have made of it. And while I believe that his delivery has obscured the beauty of much of his poetry, I am far from thinking that his poems will fall. I believe that they will have a meaning for our children, a different and perhaps a better one; and I think that what the poet sang of the steam-organ will be true of him.

> "Prophet singers will arise,
> Prophets coming after me,
> Sing my song in softer guise
> With more delicate surprise;
> I am but the pioneer
> Voice of the democracy."

BIBLIOGRAPHY

In the partial bibliography which follows I have set down only what seemed essential.

1

Mr. Lindsay's Writings

1909 (1) *The Tramp's Excuse.* Privately printed. (War Bulletin, number four. Reproduced in part in the *Village Magazine,* fourth imprint, 1925.)

1910 (2) *The Village Magazine.* Privately printed.

1912 (3) *Rhymes To Be Traded For Bread.* Privately printed. (Reissued in part in the *Village Magazine,* fourth imprint.)

1913 (4) *General William Booth Enters Into Heaven And Other Poems.* Mitchell Kennerley, New York.

1914 (5) *The Congo And Other Poems.* The Macmillan Company, New York.

(6) *Adventures While Preaching The Gospel Of Beauty.* Mitchell Kennerley, New York.

(7) The same. The Macmillan Company, New York.

1915 (8) *The Art Of The Moving Picture.* The Macmillan Company, New York.

1916 (9) *A Handy Guide For Beggars.* The Macmillan Company, New York.

(10) *A Letter About My Four Programmes.* Privately printed brochure. Interesting for discussion of the Higher Vaudeville.

(11) *General William Booth Enters Into Heaven And Other Poems.*

BIBLIOGRAPHY

The Macmillan Company, New York. Similar to item number 4.

1917 (12) *The Chinese Nightingale And Other Poems.* The Macmillan Company, New York.

1919 (13) *General William Booth Enters Into Heaven And Other Poems.* Chatto & Windus, London. Similar to item number 11. Five hundred copies struck from the American plates and imported unbound into England. Preface by Robert Nichols and letter from John Masefield.

1920 (14) *The Golden Whales Of California And Other Rhymes In The American Language.* The Macmillan Company, New York.

(15) *The Daniel Jazz.* George Bell & Sons, London.

(16) *The Village Magazine,* second imprint. Privately printed. Contains most of what appeared in the first imprint, some new material, and an invaluable index which is really a commentary.

(17) *The Golden Book Of Springfield.* The Macmillan Company, New York.

1922 (18) *The Art of The Moving Picture,* revised edition. The Macmillan Company, New York.

1923 (19) *Going-To-The-Sun.* D. Appleton & Company, New York.

(20) *Collected Poems.* The Macmillan Company, New York.

1925 (21) *Collected Poems,* new edition. The Macmillan Company, New York. Contains additional poems and preface, and drawings reproduced from the *Village Magazine.*

(22) *The Village Magazine,* third imprint. Privately printed.

(23) *The Village Magazine,* fourth imprint. Privately printed. Contains virtually all that had appeared in the three earlier imprints and much additional matter. Unique and indispensable.

1926 (24) *Going-To-The-Stars.* D. Appleton & Company, New York.

(25) *The Candle In The Cabin.* D. Appleton & Company, New York.

(26) *What It Means To Be A Poet In America.* Saturday Evening Post, November 13, 1926.

2

Criticism

An Illinois Art Revivalist, by Edward J. Wheeler, Current Literature, March, **1911.**

A Vagabond Poet, by P. C. Macfarlane, Colliers, September 6, 1913.

Mr. Vachel Lindsay, Dial, October 16, 1914.

Vachel Lindsay, by Francis Hackett, New Republic, November 18, 1916.

Contemporary Poetry, by Jessie B. Rittenhouse, Bookman, January, 1918.

Advance of English Poetry In The Twentieth Century, Part VII, by William Lyon Phelps, Bookman, April, 1918.

Vachel Lindsay Sees A New Heaven, Current Opinion, September, 1920.

Mr. Vachel Lindsay Explains America, Living Age, December 11, 1920.

Literary Portraits, by Christopher Morley, Bookman, August, 1921.

The Rodin Of American Poetry, by Glenn Frank, Century, August, 1921.

Vachel Lindsay A Folk Poet, by P. J. Benjamin, Survey, October 15, 1921.

BIBLIOGRAPHY

Salvation With Jazz, by Carl Van Doren, Century, April, 1923.

Vachel Lindsay, by Harriet Monroe, Poetry, May, 1924.

Vachel Lindsay, by Edgar Lee Masters, Bookman, October, 1926.

Vachel Lindsay In Quest Of His Youth, by Helen F. McMillin, Boston Evening Transcript, January 22, 1927.

See also:

The New Era In America Poetry, by Louis Untermeyer, Henry Holt & Company, New York, 1919.

The New Voices, by Marguerite Wilkinson, The Macmillan Company, New York, 1919.

Tramping With A Poet In The Rockies, by Stephen Graham, D. Appleton & Company, New York, 1922.

A Critical Fable (by Amy Lowell), Houghton, Mifflin & Company, Boston, 1922.